ch

The Right Place, The Right Time!

The Right Place,

The Right Time!

Tales of Chicago Symphony Days

Donald Peck

Indiana University Press
Bloomington and Indianapolis

This book is a publication of

Indiana University Press
601 North Morton Street
Bloomington, IN 47404-3797 USA

http://iupress.indiana.edu

Telephone orders	800-842-6796
Fax orders	812-855-7931
Orders by e-mail	iuporder@indiana.edu

The paper used in this publication meets the minimum
requirements of American National Standard for
Information Sciences—Permanence of Paper for
Printed Library Materials, ANSI Z39.48-1984.

Manufactured in the United States of America

Library of Congress Cataloging-in-Publication Data

Peck, Donald.
  The right place, the right time! : tales of Chicago Symphony
days / Donald Peck.
    p. cm.
  Includes discography (p.   ) and index.
  ISBN-13: 978-0-253-34914-9 (cloth)
  1. Peck, Donald. 2. Flutists—United States—Biography. 3.
Chicago Symphony Orchestra. I. Title.
  ML419.P477A3 2007
  788.3'2092—dc22
  [B]
                                    2006103063

1 2 3 4 5 12 11 10 09 08 07

Contents

Prelude: Etude on a Life in Music

As I look back on my career, it almost seems like it was an experience of someone else. How was a little boy from a little town (Yakima, Washington) able to meet some wonderful people, some famous musical artists, and—most astonishing of all—a large part of the world? This is a source of amazement to me. Of course, there were some devastating moments, such as we all have in our lives, but in retrospect I see that just going with the flow was actually the thing to do. I came to believe that we should follow our fate and not try to make it.

I also can't forget the three hundred recordings by the Chicago Symphony Orchestra of which I was a part, nor the excitement of walking out of a hotel in numerous cities of the world and knowing my way around, which way to turn to get to that restaurant, or to that shop. The little Yakima boy knows where he is in Vienna, Berlin, Paris, London, Cologne, Sydney, Tokyo, and more, as well as all of the major cities of the United States and Canada. Of course, I was playing concerts in those cities with a superb orchestra, which gave us a kinship with the people who lived there.

With the reputation of the orchestra expanding in the '70s, many of the players were invited to give solo performances in various other cities. I was very busy doing "outside" engagements. With forty performances of the Mozart Concerto for flute and harp, with five different harpists, I felt I had achieved something beyond my imagination. I followed the flow.

Our genes must have imbued us with a natural musical talent. We didn't make that, but we did have to develop it. I see that we all were driven by some inner impulse. We had to be dedicated, to study our music and instruments throughout our careers. This impulse, too, may have been a talent inside of us that was brought out by our upbringing. It is of no credit to us; we just followed our fate.

So, how about traversing this journey of mine, filled with exciting stories and amusing tales? It's not all about music, but about living, and people, and the world, our wonderful world, with of course, a touch of music thrown in.

Acknowledgments

I would probably never have written this book had it not been for the urging and encouragement of Kathleen Goll-Wilson. At that time she was editor of *Flute Talk* magazine, for which I had written many articles. When it came time for me to leave the Chicago Symphony she suggested the book to me, stressing that the public might relish a vision of the orchestra and the times.

She was immensely helpful in keeping me focused on the topic of each chapter and with my writing in general. In addition, she was a wonderful lunch partner! I thank her so much for her literary assistance, and for her friendship.

A good friend for many years has been Dr. James Compton. At one time, Jim was on the faculty at the University of Illinois. He then went to Barcelona, Spain, for five years to assist staff at the university there. When he returned, I was nearly finished with my book. He pored over all of my writings and gave me helpful grammatical corrections, including the manner of using accents and umlauts on certain words, especially those of foreign origin. But just getting another person's point of view on the tone of the writing was a great help in clearing up some areas of the text. Thank you, Jim. I won't forget that I owe you several vodka martinis!

I could not have sifted through all of the Chicago Symphony documents to gain knowledge of events and their timing had it not been for the visionary assistance of the head of the Rosenthal Archives, Frank Villella. So much information is lost to the individual that without the Archives' reminders I might have forgotten to mention many classic incidents that occurred over my forty-two years. We all must thank Frank for his help and his very pleasant company.

The Right Place, The Right Time!

1

Music Directors

*D*uring my tenure with the Chicago Symphony Orchestra, it had four music directors: Fritz Reiner, Jean Martinon, Sir Georg Solti, and Daniel Barenboim. In addition we worked with three principal guest conductors: Carlo Maria Giulini, Claudio Abbado, and Pierre Boulez. The summer Ravinia Festival had its own chief conductors, each of whom served for some years: Seiji Ozawa, James Levine, and Christoph Eschenbach. All in all, quite a group of musical notables.

Fritz Reiner, in 1953, inherited a very fine orchestra. It was not yet a great orchestra but he proceeded to quickly make it so. It was unmatched in flexibility and variety.

Jean Martinon came on the scene in 1964, which was an unfortunate time. In orchestras throughout the United States there was bickering between management, the musicians' union, and the players. Martinon had to face these problems and yet maintain the high standards of the orchestra, which he did.

These conditions were abating in 1969 when Georg Solti assumed the music directorship. Solti made use of the orchestra's greatness to advance his own world reputation, but at the same time he took the orchestra with him in this venture, thereby making it an internationally recognized icon. It was an outstanding marriage.

An enigma was Daniel Barenboim. He was a frequent guest conductor in the '70s and '80s. We made many recordings with him in those years: Bruckner's complete symphonies, the Schumann symphonies, etc. He showed us that he was a magnificent pianist and a fine musician. We enjoyed him, as did the audiences. As a guest conductor, he was pleasant and productive. Although other artists were considered for the musical directorship after Solti, it seemed natural to most of us that Barenboim was the best choice. He was hired. But the music director Barenboim did not have the same persona that we had known for the past twenty years when he was a guest conductor.

Fritz Reiner

Dr. Reiner, as we had to address him, was a great musician and a wonderful conductor. He did instill fear in the orchestra, but perhaps that was what made us so attentive. It was said that he was a tyrant. He was not alone in that. It was the modus operandi of the day. Toscanini was a tyrant, as were Szell, Koussevitzky, Klemperer, and so on. Orchestra musicians had no say about their working conditions. Tenure didn't exist, so there was no job security. In the early '60s orchestras finally responded by forming representative committees and demanding more union backing. This story later.

Reiner always had to test a new player in the orchestra for musicianship and personality. Soon after I joined the orchestra in 1957 he scheduled Symphony no. 3, the *Eroica*, by Beethoven. In the last a movement there is a rather difficult flute solo that enters abruptly. At the first of the three concerts, Thursday evening, a few measures before this solo I gestured discreetly with my flute, hoping I could get the other woodwind players to hold the tempo so that when the solo came up I could play it with ease. Dr. Reiner took note of this and immediately began to push the tempo. Needless to say, the orchestra followed him instead of me. When we arrived at the solo the tempo was quite fast. I played it. It was fine. Friday night's concert came. Several measures before the solo Reiner began to aggressively push the tempo. By the time we got to the flute solo it was outrageously fast. I just gritted my teeth, and played it!

At Saturday evening's concert I saw Reiner on the podium waiting for the moment. He had probably plotted his scheme the whole day. He started the last movement at a supremely fast tempo and proceeded to push from there, a little here, a little more there. By the time we arrived at the solo the speed was ridiculous! This made me angry, so I gathered my focus, closed my eyes, and just played the damn thing. I will say, to Dr. Reiner's credit, that when the solo ended he looked over at me and gave me a large salute with one of his hands. Nevertheless, it was a frightening experience.

A few months later we were recording *A Night on Bare Mountain*, by Mussorgsky. It ends with a beautiful, pastoral flute solo, which to me signifies the redemption that follows the fracas with the demons on Bare Mountain. I loved this solo and wanted to be properly expressive. At the rehearsal I played it thus. Reiner stopped and banged his baton again and again on the wood of his podium. "No, no," he said. "In tempo. In TEMPO!" I was hurt and angry, since I felt that I had done a lovely job on the solo. We did it again. This time I played quite loudly and absolutely in tempo, accenting all the beats and looking at him defiantly. He didn't say a word, but one side of his mouth curled up into a bemused smile. He rather liked it that I had passed his personality test with a bit of ego. I must say, even after all these years, that that recording sounds beautiful. I was expressive, but perhaps not quite as free as in the rehearsal.

Another Mussorgsky incident occurred in *Pictures at an Exhibition*. One of our percussion players was ill so an outside player was hired, a fine percussionist from the Lyric Opera Orchestra. He came to the rehearsal and played tam-tam. At a climactic peak in the piece, Reiner stopped and mumbled softly to the player, "I can't hear the tam-tam." The percussion section was situated at the rear of the stage and often had trouble getting the word from the podium up front.

The nervous player responded, "Excuse me, Dr. Reiner, I can't hear you." Reiner answered, ever so slightly louder, "I can't hear the tam-tam." The fellow then said quite fervently, "Dr. Reiner, I can't hear you." Reiner then yelled, in the most clamorous voice that we had ever experienced, "I CAN'T HEAR THE TAM-TAM!" The player was so startled and shaken up that, as an unconscious reaction, he hit the tam-tam as hard as he possibly could! There was an incredible cacophony of sound. The rest of the orchestra players grabbed their ears, to plug them against the noise.

Reiner waited until the sound had echoed away. Then he looked to the back of the stage and said, very slowly, "I hear eet now. OUT!" That "out" meant that the guy was fired. He was out; he left the stage.

At one time the orchestra had Wednesday morning rehearsals at 9 AM instead of the usual 10 AM hour. I was living in a suburb then, River Forest. I usually drove into town. On one Wednesday I had trouble getting my car started and arrived late for the rehearsal. Reiner stopped the music and watched me slink to my flute chair in the center of the stage. "Ver vas you?" he said. I answered, "I'm sorry to be late, Dr. Reiner, but my car broke down." He looked at me for quite some time with his steely stare. Finally he spoke, with a sour tone: "Don't let it break down again."

Once a new player passed all of Reiner's tests he left you pretty much alone, as long as you continued to play well. He was even quite generous with his nods and smiles and bows. It wasn't all tyranny.

Reiner was famous for his small beat: the vest-pocket beat, it was called. Much of the time the orchestra couldn't see any beat, and the audience definitely didn't either. He conducted this way purposefully, believing that if the players had to pay more attention to see the beat, they would then be more attentive to the music that was being made by the director and other members of the orchestra. The concerts were generally wonderful, with a high musical moment in each one. At that climactic place in every concert Reiner would raise his arm over his head. All hell would break loose in the orchestra that had been playing so carefully with the small beat throughout the concert. That was the most exciting time of the evening. The audience always left the concert hall talking about that moment.

Because of a heart condition, Reiner had a much-diminished schedule the last few years of his tenure. He left Chicago in 1962 and died in November of 1963, a week before the death of President Kennedy. The wags in the music business tell that Reiner raised a storm when he arrived in the heavens because the assassination had stolen press coverage from him. Out of spite, they say, he even fired two of his pallbearers.

Making jokes about autocratic behavior is a way of relieving our tension. Nevertheless, everyone always agreed that Reiner's concerts were the absolute best presentations: musical, exciting, and expertly performed. There was no one equal to him at that time, nor is there now.

Jean Martinon

If any conductor faced insurmountable odds in taking over a music directorship, it was Jean Martinon when he came to Chicago in 1963. This was the period when orchestras all over the United States were organizing themselves to fight the dictatorial treatment by managements. Chicago musicians had extra weight to bear because the very man who had founded the American Federation of Musicians, James Petrillo, was from Chicago. Theoretically, this should have given us an edge in our managerial disputes, but it appeared to us, rightly or wrongly, as if Mr. Petrillo was indulging the orchestra management instead of helping "his" musicians.

Uppermost on the turbulent scene was the president of the board of trustees of the Chicago Symphony Orchestra, Eric Oldberg. He was used to the autocratic ways of management and was against the new idea of a players' committee, to be elected by the orchestra members to represent them to the management and to the union. To carry out his wishes, Old-berg hired as manager a second-string critic from a Chicago newspaper, Seymour Raven. Degrading events for the musicians followed one after the other.

Jean Martinon, not familiar with the United States, had to deal with these situations between the feuding parties yet at the same time attempt to produce fine music with the orchestra. At the beginning of his third season, the atmosphere was so heated and hostile that he had no choice but to fire Seymour Raven. This didn't help Martinon's relationship with Eric Oldberg. In addition, Raven's colleague on the newspaper immediately began writing negative reviews of Martinon's concerts, beginning with the very next one after Raven's dismissal. Formerly the notices had all been glowing—so much for the objectivity of the press.

Jean Martinon was a gentleman and a good conductor. He was not a show-off. He had a genuine love of music and tried to present it in an honest fashion. Some of the musicians didn't understand Martinon's civilized manner, since they had dealt with the attitude of Fritz Reiner for ten years. They found it difficult to lose their fear of the podium. A few others misinterpreted his gentlemanly behavior as weakness and attempted to promote themselves by defying his rightful musical authority. This was not a happy time for the orchestra or for Jean Martinon.

Despite the turmoil, the concerts were generally very rewarding. In particular I remember a glorious performance of Mahler's Symphony no. 10, in the first Deryck Cooke reconstruction of Mahler's sketches. These concerts of May 1966 were recorded for radio, and then issued as a CD many years later, in 1990. The next year there was a great concert with Eileen Farrell as soprano soloist in scenes from Wagner operas. Also on the program was Martinon's own Fourth Symphony, which had been commissioned by the Chicago Symphony. This was later recorded on RCA Records, coupled with Peter Mennin's Symphony no. 7.

Martinon was not well known in the United States during his first few years in Chicago, so RCA had concerns about recording with him. However, this feeling soon changed and we made thirteen records with him, encompassing twenty-one different works. Included on the list are Ravel's *Daphnis and Chloe* suite no. 2, *Mother Goose,* and *Rhapsodie espagnole;* Bartók's *Miraculous Mandarin;* Nielsen's Symphony no. 4; Frank Martin's Concerto for seven winds; and one with Benny Goodman as soloist in the two Weber Clarinet Concerti.

Since he was a composer, Martinon was aware of the contemporary music scene around the world and expanded the orchestra's repertoire and vision by introducing several outstanding compositions. But, most important, he maintained the glory of the Reiner orchestra, which certainly helped Solti when he took over in 1969. Finally, after five seasons, Jean Martinon had had enough of the turmoil. He left in 1968, going to conductorial posts in Paris and The Hague, Holland. Jean Martinon died in Paris in 1976.

Georg Solti

After Martinon's departure, Irwin Hoffman filled the position of temporary music director for one year. He then left to take over the Louisville Orchestra. Georg Solti arrived on the scene in 1969 with fanfare and ballyhoo, shouting to the city, "I am a great conductor. If you don't like me, I will leave!" I believe that this was the right approach to Chicago at that time. Solti was not about to take any of the treatment that Martinon had endured.

However, most of the problems had abated by this time, especially with the accession of the new president of the board of directors, Louis Sudler. Mr. Sudler was a prominent real-estate mogul in Chicago and a baritone singer with a lovely voice. He loved music and he loved the orchestra. He hired as general manager John Edwards, formerly with the Pittsburgh Symphony and the National Symphony of Washington, D.C. John was a fine man who also was a music lover. The president of the union had also been replaced. This team, and Solti as music director, established an entirely different atmosphere on the stage of Orchestra Hall. Solti was a bit anxious at first, but when he heard the orchestra it became clear to him that Martinon had maintained the high standard and that the musicians were cooperative. He relaxed and proceeded to put his stamp on the orchestra, in a mild way at first, gaining more stimulus as time passed.

He was determined that the Chicago Symphony Orchestra should become known worldwide. This endeavor was launched with an East Coast tour in 1970. The Carnegie Hall concert in New York featuring Mahler's Fifth Symphony was hailed as the musical event of the year and inaugurated the identification of "Solti/Chicago" as a winning combination. The orchestra's first European tour was set up for 1971, a six-week venture.

Upon arriving in Europe, we were surprised to note that the people there didn't really know Solti that well. Our principal guest conductor, Carlo Maria Giulini, who shared the concerts with Solti, was very well known and loved. Needless to say, this didn't please the maestro. In any case, the tour was a rousing success. Audiences all over Europe were stunned at the musical and personal impact that we made. (See chapter 3, "Touring the World," for the full story.) When we arrived back in Chicago the city gave us a grand parade down Michigan Avenue. It was quite an event.

The response to this tour, coupled with the reception of our Carnegie Hall concert in 1970, awakened the world to the existence of a great musical force in Chicago, Illinois. *Time* magazine put out an issue with Solti on the cover with the headline "The Hottest Baton in the West." It contained an article glorifying Solti and the orchestra.

This warmth and appreciation inspired us to try harder to be even better in the ensuing years. Solti and the orchestra had a fine symbiotic relationship that is difficult to explain. Some conductors get along with some orchestras and not others. We had a good match with Solti, and he with us.

He was perceptive and quick. If you went into his office to discuss an issue, you would summarize your speech so as to not take too much of his time. But it was amazing! After only ten words of the twenty-five you had planned, he knew exactly what was being asked. He stopped you and said, "Oh yes, my dear, I understand. Just do this. . . ." That was it, he was right, and you did it.

He was a brilliant conductor who achieved a sound of great clarity from the orchestra with his incisive beat. He was therefore a perfect director for the likes of Mahler, Strauss, Bruckner, and Wagner, whose music can sometimes sound a little thick.

Maybe as an antidote to this, he loved Debussy's *Prelude to the Afternoon of a Faun.* He always called me in to discuss this work when we were about to perform it. He referred to it as Debussy's Concerto for flute. We did it numerous times in Chicago and recorded it twice. We played it on a Japanese tour, on two East Coast tours, on two European tours, on the Russian tour, on a West Coast tour, and on and on. Finally, when we had played it in every conceivable city as part of the regular printed program, he began to use it as an encore on the tours. This was problematic, as it is difficult for the flutist to play a sensitive work like the *Faun* after a long symphonic program. But we encored it everywhere. I honestly believe that I have played this piece more than any flutist ever has, or ever will.

I finally felt that if I had to be put through such trauma, I should be rewarded in some way. I went to the management and suggested that I be given a small monetary token for my efforts, as no one else in the orchestra had to face up to this nightly pressure. They said that they would "think" about it.

Solti called me into his office a week later. "My dear," he said. "I understand that you vant to be paid some cosh for the Debussy." I admitted that I would indeed. He replied, "Oh yes, I understand, but we can't do that without making a precedent for the future. I am reluctant, but I will take it off of the encore list. Instead, we will play the Scherzo from the *Midsummer Night's Dream* by Mendelssohn." I almost fell off of my chair! That also has a long and difficult flute part. How sly of him. I did get away from the *Faun*, but I was trapped by another fairy tale, and with no remuneration.

Sir Georg's sense of humor came out quite often. At one recording session we taped Benjamin Britten's *Young Person's Guide to the Orchestra*. Later, Solti himself was to record the narration required, in English, French, German, and Italian. After several months he announced to the orchestra that the project had been canceled. No recording of the Britten would be issued. He explained, "No one can understand me in any language!"

Although he was busy with worldwide conducting dates, we never felt that Solti came to us unprepared. There was no faking, or just "getting through" the score. He amazed us one year when we gave three performances of the Schoenberg opera *Moses und Aron*, a work we later recorded. This is a twelve-tone composition with a large orchestra, a chorus, and soloists. There is nothing "usual" in the sound of it. At one concert a singer lost her place. Solti looked up from the score, motioned the piccolo not to enter yet, gave the trumpets and trombones separate cues as to when to make their entrances, and finally gave a beat for the piccolo to come in. Suddenly, all was back in order. How could he have learned that score so well? And how could he have divined the problem, and its solution, in that split second? We always spoke of this moment with awe.

Solti was constantly searching out new ways of doing things. He was never satisfied with what had been. A later rendition of Beethoven's Fifth Symphony had distinctive differences from the earlier one. He realized that his stick technique was a bit too edgy and would often say, "I beat big, but you play small." That never happens; the conductor's essence comes out of the man and his appearance, not out of what he says.

One year he decided to forego the use of the baton on certain movements, or on a whole work. This was an experiment to see if he could achieve a mellower sound and a less immediate attack from the orchestra. In Mendelssohn's Symphony no. 3 (the *Scotch* symphony), which we recorded, he conducted with no baton in the slow movement. It is amazing how the sound of the orchestra changed dramatically. The tone was darker and deeper, much more relaxed. The baton does give precision but it also gives a bit of an edge. Solti had the right idea, but we got into trouble when Janet Baker came to sing Elgar's *Sea Pictures*.

No baton was used throughout the complete work. We knew the Mendelssohn Symphony no. 3 very well, but the Elgar we had never played. It was surprising that, as stubbornly accurate as Solti was when using the baton, he was completely unclear without it. He mooned with his hands, all over the podium. We didn't know where he was. If we had known the music well, we would have just listened to each other and played accordingly. But this was difficult, not knowing what to listen for. I imagine that out in the hall it was a voluptuous performance, since no one was entering on a musical line with punch; we just slid in uncertainly. Only after realizing that we might be in the correct place did we then expand our sound. Maybe Solti purposefully conducted that way to achieve this effect, but I doubt it.

We made many recordings with Solti: all of the Mahler symphonies, some twice; all of the Bruckner symphonies; the Beethoven symphonies, twice; the Brahms symphonies; many Shostakovich symphonies; five operas, cantatas, requiems, and on and on (see chapter 10, "Making Recordings"). The concerts, wherever we played, were sold out. The audience response was overwhelming. We enjoyed the performances and felt rewarded and appreciated. It was a very good time.

Daniel Barenboim

When the time came to replace Solti, the orchestra management was faced with a difficult decision, since there were few candidates of quality. A vote of the orchestra members was taken and Barenboim received a small majority, followed by Claudio Abbado and Riccardo Chailly. The job was offered to Barenboim. He took it. But the Daniel Barenboim who assumed the position of music director in 1991 was a different D. B. than we had known as a guest conductor.

He immediately wanted to change everything that had been, including the seating of the orchestra sections on the stage, the sound of the orchestra, the attitude toward music making, the programming, etc., etc. He chose to forget that the orchestra had been one of the top three symphonic ensembles in the world for the past twenty-two years. With this posture he gave a demeaning experience to the players, who were outright offended.

As a pianist, Barenboim is truly amazing. When he plays, you never hear the chords being pounded from the keyboard. They float out like the sound of a great orchestra. My first experience with Daniel Barenboim was in 1956 when I was playing principal flute with the Kansas City Philharmonic Orchestra. He was a teenager and arrived as piano soloist.

Years later, when he was music director of the Chicago Symphony, he and I were having a social conversation. I mentioned the Kansas City concert. I told him how impressed we were with his rendition of the Beethoven Third Concerto. Without any hesitation he said, "Fine, except I played the Kabalevsky Third Piano Concerto." I felt that he had to be wrong but I kept my mouth shut. I rushed home. In a closet of old programs I found the one from 1956 in Kansas City. I was amazed. It *was* the Kabalevsky Piano Concerto! He had immediately known what he had played back in 1956! I think amazed isn't strong enough. I was flabbergasted. As I sometimes say, conductors often have incredible brains.

"Danny," as we called him away in the dressing room, had a sly sense of humor that was manifest when he was in a positive mood. On a tour of Japan with Solti in 1986 Barenboim did some of the concerts, one of which was in Toyota City, home of the car manufacturer. That company treated us to a grand dinner party. Barenboim gave a witty little talk to the crowd that evening, saying how pleased we were to be in Japan, where they named us the greatest orchestra in the world. And we were especially happy to be giving a concert in Toyota City, which had the greatest carmaker in the world. You can imagine the ovation-din that followed!

On occasion he performed Mozart piano concerti with the CSO while conducting from the keyboard. With inspiring interplay between soloist and the orchestra, these were fine musical performances. Unfortunately, when conducting the orchestra from the podium he was not always able to achieve this result. The performances were often without structure, a bit meandering. We first noticed this trait in Barenboim when he was sharing the concerts with Solti on the tour of Japan.

A large work, or indeed a whole concert, needs pacing so as to lead clearly to one moment of final triumph, a *raison d'étre*. A major plan must exist or the vehicle is merely banal. The "inspiration of the moment" must not kill the larger plot. We learned this in the days of Fritz Reiner and continued with Sir Georg Solti, when the players were allowed some leeway in phrasing at the repetition of each work, but the major musical plan was always there.

This was not the case with Barenboim. There were some fine concerts, but the general level was not as high as it had been, which created a dour atmosphere and caused the orchestra to feel unappreciated. The quality of the performances then suffered even more: never bad, just not quite "there."

In the late '90s Claudio Abbado left the music directorship of the Berlin Philharmonic Orchestra. Many people argued that Barenboim might get this position, and certainly we felt that he wanted it. He made his home in Berlin. He was the director of the Berlin Staatsoper and its orchestra. He was often a guest conductor of the Berlin Philharmonic. Those players knew him well. As it happened, they chose someone quite different, musically and personally: Simon Rattle, from England. So Barenboim renewed his contract in Chicago.

It is difficult to follow someone who is a great success, as Martinon found succeeding Reiner, and Barenboim when taking over after Solti. The Chicago Symphony Orchestra had appreciated Daniel Barenboim during his many years as a guest conductor, although he was with us for only a few weeks every other season or so. We realized that he had a keen mind and was a knowledgeable musician. Admittedly, it is the privilege of the music director to make changes. However, Daniel Barenboim, and the orchestra, would have been much better off if he had achieved his aims at a slower pace and with a gesture of respect for what had been. He departed from the directorship in June of 2006.

2

Staff Conductors

*A*s the orchestra seasons throughout the country became longer and more complex, many music directors reasoned that they should not spend too many weeks per year in one city. Solti commented that the orchestra would tire of him, and perhaps the audiences too, and that he might become stale. He therefore decided that he would do twelve subscription weeks of the thirty-two-week season, and four weeks of touring. In the other weeks, we would have guest conductors.

The management felt that the season should have a broader foundation of conducting staff, so a new position was introduced for the Chicago Symphony Orchestra, that of principal guest conductor. It was to be offered to a world-renowned figure who would direct four to six weeks each season but not have to deal with the management business handled by the music director. This individual could record with the orchestra as if it were his group. I worked with three of these gentlemen: Carlo Maria Giulini, Claudio Abbado, and Pierre Boulez.

Carlo Maria Giulini

The first conductor to hold the position was Carlo Maria Giulini, from Italy, beginning in 1969, the same year that Georg Solti became music director. They were a perfect contrast to each other, Solti with his clear, brilliant, sky-blue tone and Giulini with his deep maroon, emotional sound. Although he held a baton in his right hand, he might as well not have, since he didn't generally conduct with it. He extended his arms from his body and gestured with a fluid, supple physical outflow. In our usual "lighten the atmosphere" manner, we jokingly said that in music school he had to hold two watermelons when conducting, one under each arm.

He was always very aware of what was happening. At one concert when a famous violinist playing the Brahms Violin Concerto got momentarily separated from the orchestral accompaniment, Giulini sharpened his eyes and gave a few quick, clear flicks of his baton. All was immediately back on course.

The man had a spiritual quality that affected the orchestra and the audience as soon as he walked on stage. When he started the program it was as though an oracle were speaking. His tempos tended to be slower than usual, but he created such a strong line of melody that the phrases never sagged. He was one of the few who could end a slow final movement of a work and still have a strong hold on the ears and emotions of the audience. After the finale of Mahler's Symphony no. 9 there was not a sound in the hall for many a second, as the audience came back to earth after the musical ascent. Giulini just stood there with his eyes closed. Then a few bits of applause began, and more and more, and finally it became an ovation of the highest order.

I was fortunate to perform as soloist on two series of concerts with Giulini. One year we were performing the Mozart Concerto no. 1 in G Major, and another time a contemporary piece, Sonata da Concerto, by the Italian, Giorgio Federico Ghedini. It is not often that one has a conductor of such sensitivity as a colleague. Even if I changed each performance in certain ways, Giulini was always there, and immediately adjusted the accompaniment to fit the solo.

It was both a musical and a personal pleasure when this man came to Chicago. He gave up the title of principal guest conductor after his third season, in 1972, but returned for a few years to guest conduct, during which time we made a long list of recordings with him for EMI, DG, and RCA. More of this in chapter 10, "Making Recordings."

In 1978 he took over as musical director of the Los Angeles Philharmonic. We felt that this was a mistake, as the seasonal planning, the orchestral hiring, the program building, the dealings with management and players on a business level did not seem to be a part of his personality. I believe that this proved to be true, as after only a few years he resigned and returned to Italy.

He was invited back to guest conduct in Chicago but we never saw him again. His wife was not well and did not want to travel, so his appearances were limited to Europe, most prominently in Vienna, Berlin, and London. He died in Brescia, Italy, on June 14, 2005.

Claudio Abbado

After Giulini left for Los Angeles in the spring of 1978, Claudio Abbado came to replace him in the fall of that year, holding the title for three seasons. In his earlier years he had been coached at the Tanglewood Festival, so he knew and appreciated the United States. He was well known in Europe. He had been music director of the La Scala Opera in Milan and later went to the London Symphony Orchestra as primary conductor. Like Barenboim, Abbado was a frequent guest conductor of our orchestra over the years and recorded with us on many occasions: the Mahler Symphonies nos. 1, 2, 5, 6, and 7; the complete Tchaikovsky symphonies; and many more works (see chapter 10).

The CSO was happy when he was hired as principal guest conductor, as he seemed a natural for the position after the departure of Giulini. He came to the rehearsals with the scores extremely well prepared. It was clear what he wanted out of them and how he would ask us to achieve it. The downside was that he always thought of them in the same way, with the same approach, not leaving room for inspiration, as I describe in chapter 3, "Touring the World," when I discuss Abbado and Mahler's Symphony no. 7.

Maybe because of this, his rehearsals could be tedious and his requests were intoned in a soft, flat voice, with no vitality or spark. One of his most-used phrases was given in a low mumble, barely audible. He would say, blurrily, "nodda gedda," meaning "not together." This was typical, and also made for a few laughs in the locker room. So his rehearsals seemed much longer than the time allowed or than those of some other conductors. Nevertheless, he was a gentleman, somewhat low-key off the podium, friendly and quietly witty. His non-pushy attitude evoked a lovely sound from the orchestra, with no forcing anywhere and a genteel approach to attacks. It was very civilized, calming down the brass and making the strings more flexible.

One concert in 1977 featured the music of Prokofiev: the *Lieutenant Kije* and *Scythian* suites. These were recorded on DG and expressed the epitome of the Abbado tone. That element made him, to us, the ideal conductor to program some contemporary music, which at times can be unbeautiful. Bartók's work is no longer considered modern music, but at one time it was. This was particularly true of his Piano Concerti no. 1 and no. 2. Performing and recording these with Abbado and Pollini as soloist, in 1977, we had an entirely new experience of twentieth-century music. The tonal edges were smoothed off and replaced with lyricism. It was still bright and exciting but in a civil way. I learned a lot from this and discussed it with him one year when Bruno Maderna was coming to conduct, programming a flute solo, Serenata for flute and orchestra by van Vlijmen. Abbado suggested that I forget about all the non-musical scribbles on the page and try to find an expressive quality of peace and songfulness, like an aria at the opera. I did this and was amazed at the change it made in my flute tone, in the music, and in its acceptance by the audience. I used his idea many times through the years when confronted with some anti-music music.

But even he couldn't save a work he brought one year, *Gruppen*, by Karlheinz Stockhausen. It used three orchestras strewn about the stage, with three conductors: Abbado, Matthias Bamert, and Henry Mazer. It didn't matter what notes anyone played, or at what place they played them, or with what kind of tone, or at what dynamic level, in tune or out of tune. Even with Abbado's lovely orchestra tone he couldn't rescue this one. With three orchestras screaming out musical obscenities, which had no connection with each other, it was positively laughable. The audience was less amused, as they had paid money for their tickets—to hear what? As sensitive and brilliant a man as Abbado is, at that time those qualities were not in evidence. He was sweet enough to agree with us backstage, later, that perhaps experimental music belongs in a university setting rather than in an established temple of art/music.

A contemporary work that has joined the regular repertoire is the opera *Wozzeck*, by Alban Berg. In spite of some thorny moments, it has many glorious ones, like Maria's "Remorse" aria in act 3. Abbado scheduled this for one season, arriving with no score. He was doing it from memory! Although he knew it very well, we felt overly challenged and worried. What if one of the singers had gotten lost; would Abbado have been able to get everything back in place? In any case, all went well, and we breathed again. In the late '80s Solti announced his retirement from his position as music director. A new person had to be found. The poll of the orchestra did favor Barenboim slightly, but Abbado was very high in the count. We had the feeling that he wanted the position. He may have been unhappy that he didn't get it, but this probably passed quickly as he soon became music director of the Berlin Philharmonic, another highly rated orchestra.

Pierre Boulez

The next gentleman to assume the position of principal guest conductor was Pierre Boulez, in 1995. He and music director Daniel Barenboim had been friends in Paris when D. B. controlled the Paris Orchestra for fifteen years, so this was a natural choice. Boulez had conducted us many years ago, when he was music director of the New York Philharmonic. It was not an entirely pleasant occasion, as he was anxious and edgy, though always a fine musician. We attributed this behavior to difficult circumstances in New York, which he left soon after. When he returned to guest conduct us ten years later, the stress of that situation was over and he was an entirely different man: mellow, relaxed, and friendly, making wonderful music. We were happy that he accepted the offer from our management.

Boulez doesn't use a baton when he conducts. He beats very clearly with no showy embellishments, and clarity is what he achieves from us. We have performed Mahler's Ninth Symphony at many concerts and recorded it three times with different conductors, including Boulez. To us it usually seemed powerful, heavy, expressive, and a bit thick. What a change when Boulez conducted it! It actually had clarity. One could hear all of the parts, not just an orgy of opulence. He was the perfect foil for Barenboim, as Giulini was for Solti.

Boulez is a composer, so perhaps that is the reason he has chosen to concentrate on the music of the twentieth century. Recently he has ventured into a more Romantic aspect of orchestral sound with the recording in Chicago of Richard Strauss's *Also sprach Zarathustra*. We have no memory of him conducting any of his own music with us, although other conductors have done so, frequently Daniel Barenboim.

As much as we appreciate Gentleman Pierre, the orchestra in general does not take to his music. It is very technical, with no expression that we have been able to perceive. A slightly naughty comment has been made that he is writing from a computer, without a computer. Several years ago he composed a sonata for flute and piano. I immediately bought a copy. I tried it and felt that I was too young to grasp it. I put it away for four years and tried it again, but found nothing there to interest me. I filed it away again. This went on every few years for a decade. I finally decided that I *had* to perform it. At the rehearsal with the pianist we just looked at each other. It didn't matter what we played, or when we played it. The piano would have five notes on a beat and the flute six notes, or four and seven, or whatever. It sounded as though we were warming up the instruments and playing nothing. I put it away again. I leave it "put away" except when someone brings it in for a coaching!

On the podium he is a different man. There, he maintains a proper posture, keeping everything ship-shape, yet he encourages and allows the orchestra to express itself musically. It is the combination of these two approaches that develops exciting concerts. We have made numerous recordings with him. These are discussed in chapter 10, "Making Recordings." He has now been returning to Chicago each season for twelve years.

The Ravinia Festival

The summer home of the Chicago Symphony Orchestra is situated amongst a series of upscale, posh suburbs along Lake Michigan, twenty-five miles north of downtown Chicago. It is called the Ravinia Festival. It was a private estate that was donated to the Ravinia Festival Association with the stipulation that it be dedicated to music, principally with the Chicago Symphony.

The area is approximately six blocks square. Originally the concerts were presented in a huge tent that was constructed each summer. In the late '40s an auditorium was built with a roof but with open sides. This was re-done in the '70s to be an impressive 3000-seat pavilion, again open on the sides. The sound is amplified out to the grand lawn spaces around the building so music lovers can enjoy a dinner and bottles of wine while listening to the concert and communing with nature. A smaller 750-seat theater, the Murray, is used for chamber music and recitals. In addition, an elegant dining room was erected in the '80s so a special lunch or dinner might be partaken of before the concerts; it is altogether a civilized space.

In the '50s, when I first played at Ravinia, the season was only six weeks long. There were four concerts every week, each with a different program, one rehearsal per program. This made for a lot of music in a short time. Fortunately at that time, many fine conductors were available, with a different one each week. A regular each summer was Pierre Monteux. Others we saw more than once were André Cluytens, Igor Stravinsky, Sir William Walton, Paul Hindemith, Georg Solti (his first appearance with the CSO), Eugene Ormandy, Sir Thomas Beecham, and many more. In the mid-1960s, when the complete orchestra contract was expanded to fifty-two weeks, Ravinia upped its summer presentations to eight weeks, with three concerts per week.

Seiji Ozawa

In 1964 the Festival Association decided to engage a principal conductor for the Ravinia Festival, who would stay for two or three weeks instead of the usual one week. That year Seiji Ozawa was hired for this position. He held it through the summer of 1968.

He was a very young man at that time, still coaching with Serge Koussevitzky at the Tanglewood Festival Institute. He came to rehearsals with knowledge of the scores but with no direction as to their achievement. He conducted clearly, with good tempi, and listened carefully to us. By the concert, he had picked up the musical aura that we had presented to him at the rehearsals. He added a bit of his own dash and usually came through with outstanding concerts. It was interesting to us, and maybe a bit of an ego builder, that most of the music at our concerts he had never done before. In a way, we were the teachers. He picked up an interpretation from our performances and went on from there to expand and personalize his later presentations of those works.

The orchestra enjoyed working with him. He was vibrant, witty, and appreciative of the players, often featuring them in his programming. With him I performed the Bach Brandenburg Concerto no. 2, Martinu's Concerto for flute and violin, Berio's Serenata for flute and fourteen instruments, and Mozart's Concerto for flute and harp. Chapter 10 gives the long list of our tapings with him on RCA and EMI.

Often returning to his home in Japan to conduct a major symphony orchestra in Tokyo, Ozawa was music director of the Toronto Symphony Orchestra from 1965 to 1969, of the San Francisco Symphony from '69 to '78, and then of the Boston Symphony Orchestra until 2002. He next went to the Vienna State Opera as artistic director and conductor. All in all, not a bad resume.

James Levine

In the summer of 1971, twenty-eight-year-old James Levine was asked to fill in at Ravinia on short notice for a cancellation by Istvan Kertesz. He was conducting at the Aspen Music Festival that summer as a change of pace from his winter position as assistant conductor of the Cleveland Orchestra. He was hired for the next summer as principal conductor at Ravinia, a title that he kept for twenty years. The Metropolitan Opera signed him as principal conductor in 1973, and in 1976 made him artistic director, a position he still holds.

Coming to Ravinia at such a young age, he reminded us of Seiji Ozawa, as Levine was also musical, smart, and quick. He too had learned the musical scores, but had not yet devised their interpretations. He gleaned a lot from us by listening to our expression of the musical lines. We undoubtedly influenced his career, but his major influence was probably George Szell, under whom he worked as assistant conductor of the Cleveland Orchestra for several years. This became apparent to us a few years later when he seemed to have arrived at his own interpretive stage.

When the music that he was conducting had a story, like an opera or a symphonic poem, he was very good at expressing those emotions. But when it was just pure music with no built-in tale, as with a Beethoven or Schumann symphony, he followed the technical line of George Szell or Arturo Toscanini by making the performance fast and frenetic, with little emotional content. Fortunately we performed, and recorded, many orchestral poems with him, including Holst's *The Planets* and Mendelssohn's *A Midsummer Night's Dream*. He also performed complete operas with us, including Strauss's *Ariadne auf Naxos*, Berlioz's *Les Troyens*, Mozart, and Wagner, which were all very satisfying.

He wanted us to call him "Jimmy," as he asked everyone worldwide to do. It was charming at first, but I suppose that mannerisms do become cloying after a time, and he had many: like the towel that he kept thrown over his shoulders at rehearsals, and his constant comment, "fabulous, folks." His manner was attractive in the beginning, but finally we felt it was not to be trusted. It was only acting. One year some orchestra members teamed up to instigate a plot. They asked us to come to a rehearsal wearing towels over our shoulders. I would estimate that seventy of us did this. He walked onto the stage, climbed to the podium, saw us, and looked flabbergasted. He laughed and laughed. But then, guess what he said? "Fabulous, folks!"

The famed Austrian singer Elizabeth Schwartzkopf came to Ravinia to perform Mahler's *Das Lied von der Erde*. Because of the amplification out to the lawn areas, the balance on the stage was sometimes inaccurate. We had grown used to this, but Schwartzkopf did not know about it. During a gorgeous duet between vocalist and flute in the last movement she turned to Jimmy and told him that the flute was too loud. I had played this work many times and at that point had recorded it twice, with Reiner and Solti, so I really *did* know what I was doing. Jimmy looked up at me, cautiously. With a twinkle in his eye he said to her, "Oh no, I'm not going to touch that one." I wonder if I had a reputation. In any case, I loved him for that reply.

I performed, with Jimmy at the piano, the Bach Brandenburg Concerti nos. 2, 4, and 5, recording 2 and 5. I also did the Mozart Flute Concerto no. 2 in D Major, and the Telemann Suite in a minor for flute and strings. The orchestra had a large recording schedule with Levine during that year, which is described in chapter 10.

His career expanded prodigiously in the '80s, with engagements throughout the world, notably at the Bayreuth Festival and in Berlin and Munich. We were pleased that an American was finally getting noticed, as Leonard Bernstein was no longer around. But it led to a bit of a problem at Ravinia. Jimmy would come rushing into Chicago with very little time to spare before the rehearsal. It was obvious that he had not studied the scores at this time—too busy elsewhere? So at the rehearsal he would conduct for a short time and stop. He would make some irrelevant comment and ask us to go to a rehearsal letter back a bit. He would start again and this time go a little farther before he stopped—another inane remark, and then back. And so on, and so on. Any of these comments could have been replaced with a gesture of his hand. He was doing this routine so as to re-learn the score—on our time, thank you very much. But by the concert he had accomplished his purpose and the programs were usually quite good, even with an orchestra that was occasionally disgruntled or feeling used.

Overall it was a good twenty years that we had with Levine, just as we appreciated our twenty-two years with Solti. There will always be ups and down in any relationship, but the downs mustn't govern the product. In retrospect, the ups won for Jimmy with our orchestra. In 2004 he went to the Boston Symphony Orchestra as music director, but still with the Metropolitan Opera.

Christoph Eschenbach

In 2003 Christoph Eschenbach became the music director of the Philadelphia Orchestra. He came to Ravinia as principal conductor soon after James Levine left and stayed through the summer of 2003. Like Daniel Barenboim, he was known to us first as a pianist, and also like Barenboim, he is indeed an outstanding keyboard artist. We felt that as a conductor he was not able to make his musical points to the orchestra, as his stick technique was not good.

For example, we didn't know his tempo in a piece since he never gave an upbeat to declare the tempo. The downbeat tells nothing. It is the upbeat that gives the speed of the work, and therefore the tempo to be played. He also wouldn't just let us play, but kept up a constant cycle of interference. Often his interpretations were very mannered and fussy, with tempos getting slower with each performance. We felt a lack of general direction to the whole performance, unlike that which Reiner and Solti had instilled in us. As it happened, the Philadelphia Orchestra did not renew his contract, so he left that music directorship at the end of the 2007–2008 symphony season.

James Conlon was hired to replace him as principal conductor of the Ravinia Festival, beginning in 2004.

3

Touring the World

*O*rchestra touring became big business in the '60s, perhaps brought into being by the recording companies and the conductors who wanted to become renowned. But it didn't harm the orchestra musicians. We garnered a bit of attention ourselves, and experienced the world.

I loved the tours—becoming familiar with famous cities, knowing where I was when I stepped outside the hotel door, which way to go to what place. This was exciting to me. Also, the very positive foreign response to our orchestra may have been a boon to local ticket sales. It made the population curious about and proud of their own.

There were some trips with Jean Martinon, but the Symphony did not tour frequently until the arrival of Solti, who made touring one of the requirements of his contract. But we did have one fabulous tour with Fritz Reiner to the East Coast in October of 1958, my second year in the orchestra. We hit many places but concentrated on Boston, New York, Philadelphia, and Washington, D.C. Today people still mention the concert in Boston to me as the greatest performance ever to be heard. And we speak of it in the same way. Reiner was at his best that night, as were we, in Berlioz's *Corsair Overture*, Brahms's Symphony no. 3, and Strauss's *Ein Heldenleben*. The look on Reiner's face during and immediately after the performance was tearful with gratitude. It showed the man as something much more than a tyrant, or a great conductor. Inside he was a gentle human being.

Our next venture was to have been a tour to Europe and the Soviet Union in the spring of 1959. Abruptly we were told that Reiner had canceled the tour. He actually had the audacity to come to a rehearsal and tell us that we wouldn't like it in Russia in the spring—"it rains." The State Department replaced us with the young Leonard Bernstein, newly appointed music director of the New York Philharmonic. His tour was a big success, helping to secure Bernstein's position in New York. As it turned out, we heard several months later that Reiner was suffering from congestive heart disease. His doctor had advised that participating in the eleven-week tour might be dangerous for him. Management didn't want to announce this, as they thought that it would be a detriment to his career.

Jean Martinon became music director in the fall of 1963. Since Oldberg, the board chairman who had formerly made the comment "the Chicago Symphony is for Chicagoans only," was no longer in office, the new personnel immediately started booking out-of-town dates. In April of 1964 the orchestra had an extensive tour of the East Coast with dates in Carnegie Hall in New York on the sixteenth and seventeenth.

Before those, we were to perform in Wilkes-Barre, Pennsylvania. Martinon had planned to do the Schoenberg Five Pieces for Orchestra in New York and wanted a "run-through" before that concert, so it fell in the lap of Wilkes-Barre. I don't think that Wilkes-Barre had ever heard of Schoenberg before that evening. He certainly didn't become one of their favorites. When it ended no one applauded. They were either asleep, or they didn't know that it had ended, or maybe they were just aghast. So Martinon gave a typical French shrug, winked at us, and walked off stage. But he did get his dress rehearsal for Carnegie Hall. We redeemed ourselves a bit after intermission when we played Beethoven's Fifth Symphony, which did get some applause.

The orchestra made its first jaunt to the West Coast May 3–27, 1965. Assistant conductor Irwin Hoffman did three of the concerts, and Jean Martinon the other nineteen. Starting in Utah, we leaped over to Southern California and worked our way through the state. Then came Portland, Seattle, Vancouver, Anchorage, Fairbanks, Winnipeg, and home. In Alaska we had two concerts in each city, so we had a few days to get a taste of the great north woods.

After one of the programs in Fairbanks I went to a party. Walking back to the hotel later, I stopped to buy a newspaper, sat down in a nearby park, and proceeded to read it, very easily, even though it was midnight! Still light—light all summer, I guess, but of course it is dark all winter.

A cute episode after another concert showed us the real flavor of Alaska. We were standing outside of the hall waiting for our transport back to the hotel when a gorgeous couple came walking by: a young lady dressed in a stunning formal gown and her handsome escort in a tuxedo. They proceeded to the parking lot, where they got into a Jeep—not a modern Jeep, but one that must have been left over from World War II. Well, you have to have *some* way of getting around during the many snowy months!

Anchorage showed us a bit of history. There had been a large earthquake some time before we arrived. The fault line had been directly under the main street of the city and parallel with it. One side of the street had all of the old buildings standing in perfect order and with a historical appearance. The other side of the street was completely flattened, with debris that had the look of a bombing raid. When we went back a few years later it had been rebuilt, but the style was more modern, making a certain conflict with the opposite side of the street.

Our last stop was Winnipeg, in Manitoba. The plane with the orchestral instruments and equipment was delayed for some reason. This was explained to the audience. They participated in the ensuing discussion, saying they would wait for it to arrive if we would then play. Instead of playing an 8 PM concert we were finally able to get on the stage at 10 PM. The audience was still there and gave huge applause when we entered the auditorium. We cut the program a bit and were able to get out by 11:30. What a wonderful audience! We always hoped that we had given them something to remember besides the delay.

As you see, by this time we were on the touring circuit. In 1966, from Feb. 20 through March 13, we made the rounds of Florida, Georgia, North and South Carolina, and Connecticut, as well as playing the now usual two concerts in New York City with Martinon conducting. On this tour we played the Frank Martin Concerto for seven winds twelve times. It made the tour quite exhausting. We recorded the work upon our return to Chicago.

In November we had an East Coast junket of thirteen cities including Boston, New York, Philadelphia, and Washington, D.C. You know what happened in '67? Right—an East Coast tour in November, with two concerts at Carnegie Hall.

Martinon left to return to Paris in the spring of 1968 to take over the French National Orchestra. Georg Solti had been hired as the new music director but wasn't coming to Chicago until October of 1969, so we had no tours during the '68–'69 season.

But in January 1970 we were in Carnegie Hall with Solti, playing Mahler's Fifth Symphony, which became our signature tune. The *New Yorker* magazine gave a rave review and a big spread about that concert, as did all the newspapers. We were overwhelmed by the acclamation. This concert made the words "Solti" and "Chicago" into a one-word amalgamation that set the standard for twenty years—Solti/Chicago!

With the Symphony having been known for some years as "the world's greatest *unknown* orchestra," the marvelous new chairman of the board, Louis Sudler, and his general manager, John Edwards, decided it was time for a grand European tour, the first in the history of the orchestra. Carlo Maria Giulini, the principal guest conductor, agreed to share the concerts with Solti. And what a tour!

Off we went on August 26, 1971, arriving in Vienna on the twenty-seventh. As a first project, we recorded Mahler's Symphony no. 8 for Decca-London records. It's a grand work with a huge orchestra, a chorus, and eight stellar soloists, an hour and twenty minutes in length. Unfortunately our management didn't feel that they could afford to transport our fabulous Chicago Symphony Chorus to Vienna for the recording, so we had to use the chorus of the Vienna State Opera. They were very good, but they did not quite reach the standard of the Chicago Symphony Chorus. However, after a few hours of listening to us play the Mahler, their earlier cool attitude did change greatly. We saw them hanging over the choir loft, observing us, as if looking at teenage idols. Very rewarding, I must say.

We recorded for four days at the Sofiensaal, which was an arena-like space—a dance hall? a show hall?—with a balcony going all around it. It was used for recording by several labels for many years, but was destroyed by fire some time later.

Finishing the recording, we began the tour in earnest. Let me list the cities and the number of concerts in each, so that you will have an idea of the huge expenditures of time, money, and artistry that this required. Edinburgh—4 concerts, Ghent—1, Brussels—1, Helsinki—1, Goteberg—1, Stockholm—2, Frankfurt—1, Hanover—1, Berlin—2, Hamburg—1, Vienna—2, Milan—3, Munich—1, Paris—2, London—2, and then home to Chicago, on October 6.

The reviews from the European press were raves, with the exception of one Berlin critic. Of the two concerts in Berlin, one was conducted by Solti and the other by Giulini, who did Beethoven's Seventh Symphony. The Berlin writer said, in effect, "how dare an AMERICAN orchestra come to GERMANY and play BEETHOVEN with an ITALIAN conductor"! Charming, isn't it?

Word of the exuberant response to our concerts had made its way back to America, and we were greeted as though we had discovered the moon. Chicagoans gave us a huge parade down Michigan Avenue. We felt like heroes. But, no rest for the weary. Off we went for a week in November with two concerts at Dartmouth, two in New York, and one in Washington, D.C. The acclaim from the audiences was awesome. They had heard about Europe. Now I know how the Beatles felt!

After this, for the next decade, the eastern tours were on our schedule every spring and fall. We always gave two, three, or four at Carnegie Hall in New York, and alternately would visit Washington, D.C., Philadelphia, Boston, Hartford, Dartmouth, Brooklyn, etc. Solti did his first West Coast tour in May of 1973. After the usual East Coast hop, we raced to Austin, Albuquerque, Phoenix, Fresno, Cupertino, San Francisco, and San Diego.

In September of 1974 we took our second European tour. Again starting in Vienna we had three days of recording, Beethoven's Symphonies nos. 6 and 7, and a concert. Then off we went to Munich, Frankfurt, Zurich, Venice, Florence, London, Paris, Amsterdam, and Brussels, often with two concerts in a city. We were scheduled for two in Venice and ended up not doing any. There was a dockworkers' strike. They would not unload our equipment, so we were given two free days in Venice.

I had been there once before on vacation and now enjoyed visiting old haunts, like the classy American Bar. It was even more interesting because we did not stay in Venice proper but across the bay, on the island of Lido, in past days a very upscale resort. We had rooms at the famous Grand Hotel des Bains, where the movie *Death in Venice* had been filmed. One day, walking north on the beach, friends and I came across a huge gun embankment, now empty and open. What an eerie feeling, though, as we found out that it had been used in World War II against Allied landings.

A quirky little event occurred in Florence, which was next on the route. Since we had no concerts in Venice and the music from both Venice and Florence was to be performed next in London, Solti decided to do most of each of those programs in just Florence. What a long concert that was, with both Beethoven's Symphony no. 3 and Mahler's Symphony no. 5 in the same concert! But the audience loved it and applauded for encores.

The year 1977 arrived and brought more of the same, plus our first tour to Japan. We crammed in a recording on June 1 and 2 of the Verdi *Requiem*, one of the few recordings that Solti made for RCA. The soloists were Leontyne Price, Janet Baker, Veriano Luchetti, and José Van Dam. We left for Tokyo in a bit of frenzy on June 3, arriving on the fifth.

Then the concerts began. We had three in Tokyo at that time. The response from the people was amazing: quiet as could be during the music, and then deafening applause! Outside the hall afterward, the fans were lined up to speak to us, to meet us, to get autographs, and to ask musical questions. A great reward for us. We then went to the city of Sapporo, on the northern island of Hokkaido, and to the southern city of Nagoya. Next were Hiroshima, Fukuoka, Ishikawa, Osaka, Niigata, and three more programs in Tokyo.

There is a rather sad tale about Hiroshima, the city hit by the first atom bomb. It was all rebuilt except for one damaged edifice they have left as a memorial. We strolled through it, looking aghast at the pictures of the bomb devastation. Our concert that evening was poorly attended, which was a shock, as every other city had been completely sold out. The response was what is called lukewarm. This was thirty years after the war ended, but the memory was obviously still alive in the city. We never returned there on future tours.

The usual East Coast tour presented itself in May of 1978 with New York and Washington, D.C., a total of five concerts. But the excitement of the year was another gala tour of Europe beginning August 26, with two, three, or four days in each city. London, Edinburgh, Lucerne, Brussels, Paris, and then the Austro-German portion with Berlin, Hanover, Hamburg, Stuttgart, Munich, and three concerts at the Salzburg Festival.

By then we were getting just a little worn on *Wiener Schnitzel, Sausage mit Sauerkraut, Wurst* and so on. At that time, the restaurants in Germany and Austria were rather one-sided in their offerings. No matter how good it was, and it was good, after two weeks we felt that it was time for a change. So we looked around Salzburg, specifically on the street where Mozart had lived and worked. It was very old and charming, with cobblestone paving. We found, on the second level of a building, a Chinese café, Hunan. We tried it, and it was very good indeed. What a welcome change! On our dates in Salzburg into the nineties, this restaurant was always there to relieve our palates. So we managed to survive Salzburg, with a few fine German-Austrian meals with which to do our duty. After all, we were in Austria!

This food-searching endeavor we utilized often "on the road." In Berlin, on the first couple of tours, we stayed at the Kempinski Hotel, on the main boulevard of West Berlin, the Kurfurstendamm. One block from the hotel is Kantstrasse, another big avenue. Turn to the left and walk one and a half blocks. On the left is a French bistro, Café de Paris, a very friendly place, with jovial help. We spoke a few words of French, a few words of German, and they indulged us by speaking English. We've been there many times.

Management gave us a rest in 1979, with only three concerts in New York in May. The following year also was more restful, with five concerts in New York in May, and a Midwest tour in August with Erich Leinsdorf conducting.

Our 1981 European jaunt, from August 25 to September 20, included all the usual places, plus three new venues: Bonn, Milan, and Amsterdam. One musical item that keeps us all very alert on tour is the fact that each concert hall has quite different acoustics. This means that musicians must constantly adjust their playing so that their instruments will sound proper in each space. Solti was very good at adjusting the tempo of the music on the program to suit the hall acoustics.

In Milan, the La Scala Opera House was where we played. It may be great for opera, but not for orchestra concerts. It gave a very dead, dry sound. Solti, therefore, took slightly faster tempi on the whole program so that the sound would not just spit into the hall with no legato connections. Solti often did the Scherzo from the *Midsummer Night's Dream* by Mendelssohn for an encore. It requires terrific breath control, nimble fingers, and a quick tongue from the flutist. When we got to the Milan encore, he took it so fast that I wondered if it was playable. It is a swift piece always, but this was preposterous! That shows you the trouble one can get into when the conductor trusts you. We came to the really difficult part near the end. I just closed my eyes, so to speak, and played the damn thing. It was a matter of pride.

The next night we performed in Amsterdam, at the Concertgebouw. This hall is very live. The string players love it, as it makes them sound plush and lush. To me, at our section of the stage, everything just sounds mushy. When it came time for the Mendelssohn, Solti took it slowly. He was right, of course, as he wanted it to be clear to the audience, and a fast tempo would have made it a muddy mess. However, how was I going to hold my breath for that nightmare-long ending? Well, needless to say, I just did it! But, whew! The wind players sitting around me nicely shuffled their feet afterward, which is the way orchestra members applaud each other. Solti looked at me and laughed in an appreciative, good-colleague way.

Back to the West Coast in January of 1982. We started in St. Louis, and went on to Salt Lake City, Tucson, Phoenix, Tempe, San Francisco, Los Angeles, Denver, and Minneapolis. There was an unhappy little problem in Salt Lake City in their new concert hall where we were playing. It had very good acoustics, but was not quite broken in as to its idiosyncrasies. The doors into the auditorium from the lobby had to be closed from backstage by the stage crew, using some type of electrical air pump. After intermission we were to play Debussy's *Prelude to the Afternoon of a Faun*, which begins with one flute playing alone, a soft, sensuous melody. We got on stage; Solti gave me the nod and I started the music. Suddenly, hissing, banging, scraping sounds permeated the hall. It was the lobby doors closing. I almost stopped playing but I continued and the noise finally stopped. Solti looked startled. It shook us all up, including the audience. We found out later that the stagehands hadn't been paying attention. They should have closed the doors as Solti made his way to the podium. The door noise would have been covered by the applause welcoming the conductor. Solti thanked me later for not stopping. The performance never really got off the ground after that unsettling beginning.

April of 1983 had the expected Carnegie Hall concerts, and in September we did a round of some smaller Midwestern cities. In January 1984, Claudio Abbado, at that time our principal guest conductor, took us on a southeastern trip including nine concerts, on which we were able to overcome the chill of the winter. This tour gave us some insight into the Abbado style.

We had nine performances of Mahler's Symphony no. 7. This is a very long, sometimes irascible work. Abbado did it exactly the same way on every concert. He had learned it technically, but then never provided it with any variety of musical inspiration. By the end of the tour it had become exceedingly boring, always the same old thing. Upon our return, we recorded it and managed to pull together to achieve a fine recording. This showed to the orchestra that a greater part of a conductor's job should be to energize the music with some atmosphere and direction, not just mandate the written notes. The notes are only the beginning, the basis. Then we must make the music.

Our European tours had always been made in the spring or autumn. Solti had the idea, however, that we should visit once during the regular concert season. So in 1985 a tour was planned for January. I never want to hear another snide remark about Chicago weather in the winter. In other words, we froze, if not quite to death, in Europe.

The tour started in Stockholm on January 12. I had been to that city twice before and had enjoyed it. Even this time was not so bad, except that the sun rose at 11 AM and set at 3 PM. The temperature almost never made it above zero. We moved on and nothing changed in Hamburg, Bonn, Düsseldorf, Frankfurt, Zurich, Madrid, Paris, Amsterdam, and Brussels, until London.

Do you think that Madrid might have been warm? Forget it. It was not Stockholm, but it was *not* warm. The city is at a high altitude, and that keeps it from having a southern-type winter. Anyhow, eventually it was February and we went to Paris. As usual in Paris, it was raining, and this was not the charming rain we hear about in the song "April in Paris." But at last we had a reprieve. This surprised us, as it was in London, where we had three days, two concerts, and pleasant weather: 59 degrees. It seemed tropical by comparison with elsewhere.

When 1986 rolled around we were off again, to Japan and somewhere new. We had two concerts in Tokyo before moving on to Nagoya, Osaka, Anjo City, Toyota City, and then three more concerts in Tokyo. The new event was our stop in Hong Kong. We were there for seven days and gave five concerts. What excitement it was to experience this new culture! We walked all over the area. The streets are lined with shops, selling mostly fine items, for which you must bargain. Never pay the price asked; the dealer doesn't expect you to. I bought a sapphire ring at a reasonable price, not really knowing how good or bad the stone might be. My jeweler in Chicago examined it very carefully and pronounced it to be one of the best sapphires he had seen. I was lucky, I guess.

We had another January tour in 1987, starting in Minneapolis—brrr. I thought I was back in Stockholm. Then quickly through the Midwest, California, Texas, and home. We hit Oklahoma—but not too hard—only Bartlesville. We saw the Frank Lloyd Wright edifice that had housed the headquarters of the H. C. Price Company. It was very attractive and of interest to us since Wright is an icon in Chicago, where he lived and worked, designing many structures. That particular building in Bartlesville is one of Wright's few skyscrapers. It was built in 1956 and is nineteen stories tall. In 2003 seven of its upper floors were transformed into a boutique hotel, named the Inn at Price Tower.

The orchestra commented for years afterward that the best tour we ever had was to Australia from February 24 to March 20, 1988. Solti shared the concerts with Michael Tilson Thomas. The travel took place with a minimum of problems and the cities were most enjoyable. But the best part was the Australian people, who are so approachable, friendly, and witty. After three days in Sydney to recover from the twenty-hour flight we moved on to go to work, first across the continent to Perth.

Perth is about the only thing in that whole area. I wondered why it was even there, but it was a charming city, and very hot. This was summer, after all, in Australia.

My pal on all of the tours was first violinist Paul Phillips. Paul and I decided to go to the beach, on the Indian Ocean. We got there. Not a soul, or a body, was in evidence. We shrugged and plopped down on our towels on the sand. But only for five minutes. This was definitely summer! It must have been at least 120 degrees. That was why the beach was empty! The sun in that part of the world is very dangerous, and people try to protect themselves from it. We ran back to the hotel and had a swim in the pool, an inside pool.

We gave three concerts and were off to Adelaide, my second favorite place in that country. This city is on the south coast, and so it is not so hot. Yes, everything is backward, hotter up north and cooler down south, on the southern side of the equator. We visited several wineries in the hills around the area but fortunately managed to stay keen enough to play the three concerts scheduled. We also visited a civilized hall of gambling. That "sport" is government-controlled in Australia, so it seems much less rowdy than in some other places. After the tour, Paul ended up $275 ahead. Me, I lost $65.

We then gave three concerts in Melbourne. I have been there on three occasions and have never been entirely fond of it. The city feels secondary to Sydney and by my observation has a chip on its shoulder about this. Their concert hall is underground. I don't mean secretive, only dug into a big hole and covered over. One might ask why? Since it is in a park area, we were told, they didn't want a building intruding on nature, so they buried it. Hmm. It was given the name Hamer Hall in 2004.

And then to Sydney, with three concerts. How I love that place! It has extensive gardens and parks in the middle of the shopping and business districts, many fine, varied restaurants, and exquisite views on a myriad of walking options. But again, I enjoy the people. Perhaps I could even live there, though there isn't much else within a 7,500-mile radius. Maybe that is what makes the people so responsive to each other.

On my two previous trips in the '70s, when I was doing recitals and classes for the Australian Radio Training Orchestra, I noticed a large, very old area on one side of the bay that had been abandoned and was in ruins. But by 1988 it had been restored and was now a great restaurant and entertainment area called The Rocks. We examined that thoroughly, with all of its Australian dishes like barramundi and Balmain bugs. They taste great; just don't look at them—ugh! Sydney has an eye-catching, glamorous building on the bay called the Sydney Opera House. The Danish architect Jorn Utzon designed it. Inside are an opera theater and a concert hall. In the guidebooks it is referred to as Australia's most famous land-mark. Our three concerts were in this concert hall.

We did our last program in Brisbane, a smaller city up north. Then, back to the U.S.A. I regretted leaving, but I returned on my own for the month of March in 2002 for recitals, master classes, and some university teaching in Newcastle and Sydney. Another joyful time.

In June, Leonard Bernstein came to guest conduct for two weeks; I say more about this elsewhere. We recorded Shostakovich's Symphonies nos. 1 and 7, which we then took to Avery Fisher Hall in New York for a concert. That was all the touring in 1988. Wasn't that enough, what with Australia?

The orchestra only went to New York, Washington, D.C., and Boston in 1989. However, I myself had an interesting journey in March, going to California to perform the Morton Gould Flute Concerto with Gould conducting, in Monterey, Carmel, and Salinas. In addition, I did a tour of Japan in June of 1989 with the Chicago Symphony Chamber Players as described in chapter 11, "Solo Dates."

In August and September 1989 the orchestra went to Europe, starting in London at the Proms Festival with Sir Georg Solti conducting. We gave two concerts, one of which was Berlioz's *The Damnation of Faust* with Anne Sofie van Otter, Richard Lewis, José Van Dam, and Peter Rose as soloists. But of even greater interest was the European debut of the glorious Chicago Symphony Chorus, a fabulous success. This concert was televised. The tape is still available in shops. What an ear-opener it was for London to hear that performance with that chorus, and the same at the Salzburg Festival two days later. The applause, loud and appreciative, went on and on. We were getting nervous that we would miss a nightcap at our favorite bar, since at that time in London the law closed the bars at 11:30 PM. However, we did make it.

It was always pleasant to be in London. The orchestra stayed at either the Park Lane Hilton Hotel or the adjacent Intercontinental Hotel, on Hyde Park. Behind these buildings is a bit of London called the Hilton Mews, a collection of small lanes criss-crossing each other, spotted with shops and quaint little eateries. How ultra-charming it was to sit outside at one of these coffee shops and watch the world walk by with grace and cultivated style. One day Paul and I saw Sofie van Otter and her husband enjoying this relaxation. They asked us to join them, which we did for a short time before heading off for more London exploration.

There are so many fascinating places to visit in London that I can't list them all, but on a grand walk I often saw the Tate Gallery of Art, St. Paul's

Cathedral, the Covent Garden opera district, the shopping on Regent and Oxford Streets, Piccadilly Circus (a traffic circle with a statue of Eros), Knightsbridge Road (a casual area with pleasant bars), the Soho theater district, and Buckingham Palace. Are you tired?

Salzburg followed the London concerts, again with the *Damnation of Faust*, after which the chorus went home. The orchestra continued on the tour to seven of the usual cities plus two new ones, Copenhagen and Gothenburg.

Having been in Japan in June of 1989 doing the chamber music concerts, I now really felt worldly, as I was back there again in April of 1990 with the orchestra. Solti and Barenboim shared the concerts. We had six programs in Tokyo and six more in five other cities. On several of the tours we stayed at the wonderful Okura Hotel in Tokyo. This is on a hill, up a distance from the shopping area called the Ginza, with its myriad of huge, lavish department stores. We could leave the hotel, turn right, and walk to the bottom of the hill, six blocks or so. Directly in front of us would be the impressive Imperial Palace, surrounded by an enormous moat. If we turned right again, after a few more blocks we entered the Ginza.

Or we could leave the hotel, continue straight ahead, and enter a small park with a path going down the hill to a large plaza on which reigned Suntory Hall, where we played some of our concerts in Tokyo. The other hall in Tokyo where we performed was called Bunka Kaikan. It was quite a distance from the hotel, so we had special buses to take us there. Traffic was so dense, however, that I usually took the subway when going to this hall.

Subway travel in central Tokyo was not difficult. The stops all had their names posted in Japanese and English. The cars were clean and very quiet. However, one never goes on the subway during the rush hour, as the trains are jammed. At every stop new patrons are pushing and forcing their way on board. This seemed so out of character with the usual politeness of the Japanese. No doubt it was just a necessary evil because of the large number of passengers during rush hour. Another subway alert! Away from the central area, the station signs are only in Japanese with no English subtitles. It can be scary, so brush up on your Japanese!

The orchestra had another unusual journey in 1990, in November and December. Why this tour was scheduled during those winter months is still a point of discussion, as the tour was basically to Russia. At that time Russia was still the USSR. We started in Leningrad, which is now back to being St. Petersburg. The plane was parked miles from the terminal building, so it took us forever to be transported there. That space itself had all the glamour of an ancient barn. It took over two hours for customs and baggage personnel to allow us to leave the area. And then, another long bus ride into the city.

We stayed at the Pribaltiskaya Hotel, which was some distance from downtown, on the Gulf of Finland. It looked impressive from the outside, but as we walked in through the marble-floored lobby we heard, and felt, sand crunching under our shoes. Cleaning was apparently not always a priority at that time in the USSR. Nevertheless, my room was pleasant, if small, and at least it was heated. It was well below zero outside.

We began work the next day, recording Bruckner's Symphony no. 8 in the local auditorium, the Bolshoi Hall of the Philharmonie. That took a day and a half. On the evening of the second day we had our first concert, at which we played Mahler's Symphony no. 5, with Debussy's *Afternoon of a Faun* as an encore. Finally came a free morning. We took a tour into the city, but especially to the famous Hermitage Museum. It had a grand display of famous works of art, perhaps left over from the days of the tsars. Another concert that evening, Bruckner's Symphony no. 8, again with the *Faun* as an encore.

We then left Leningrad on an overnight train to Moscow. It was not a new train. Some of the cars were freezing while others were roasting. I lucked out and got a medium-temperature unit. We each had a tiny little room for sleeping. About 4 AM I awoke and raised my window blind to view the landscape.

It was devastating! Deep snow was piled over miles of tundra. Occasionally I would see a small shack huddling in the snow, with a metal chimney and a stream of smoke floating out of it. I wondered what it was like inside the house, and who might be living there. I felt very thankful for my life. Incidentally, it was November 23, 1990, Thanksgiving Day.

We arrived in Moscow at noon on the twenty-third. We felt relieved that we had the rest of the day free. That evening we had a special Thanksgiving Day dinner served us at the hotel, the Mezhdunarodnay. The dinner was beef stroganoff. Happy Thanksgiving!

Question—can anyone tell me how to pronounce the name of the hotel? By comparison with some others it was an upscale residence, built along the Moscow River. Nevertheless, half of the rooms didn't have shades or drapes. Another half didn't have shower curtains. All of the faucets spewed water that was rusty, musty, murky, and muddy. Communism in action!

The next day Paul Phillips and I went for a walk through the city. The people looked at us warily and kept their distance. Paul wore his earmuffs. He was stared at as though he were a monster. I don't think that they had ever seen earmuffs. They no doubt thought that his real ears were huge with black fur on them.

We decided to take a taxi back to the hotel. The driver didn't want rubles. He wanted American dollars, or even better, Marlboro cigarettes. People had clued us in on this issue, so we had brought cigarettes to Russia, though neither of us smoked. When we gave him some one-dollar bills we had to sneak them up to him between the break in the upholstery. He immediately hid them under his seat. What a life to be living!

The concert that evening, at the Great Hall of the Conservatory, was Mahler's Fifth Symphony with *Afternoon of a Faun* as an encore. On Monday, November 26, we gave another concert, Bruckner's Eighth Symphony, and again *Faun* as an encore.

We left Moscow on Tuesday the twenty-seventh. As we were flying to Budapest and leaving Russian airspace, Solti got on the airplane speaker system and said, "Well, my dears, we are leaving Russia. Thank gott!"

What a change we experienced when we landed in Budapest. The people were most helpful and friendly, a different world from Russia. We couldn't believe that the country was under the Communist boot.

The area is really two cities, Buda and Pest, on opposite sides of the Danube River. Our hotel was the Thermal Hotel Helia. It looked to be fairly new. It was warm and bright, and the water was clean! Our concert on the twenty-eighth of November was a welcome change from the recent Bruckner and Mahler. We played an all-Bartók program. This gentleman was Hungarian, as was Solti. But we had the usual *Afternoon of a Faun* as an encore. This concert was taped and televised.

Vienna was the final stop, on November 29, with one concert the next day. Back to Mahler's Fifth. It was recorded live at the performance, our second recording of the work with Solti. Guess what the encore was? On December 1 we flew home.

In spite of being disturbed by Communist Russia and irritated by many events on this tour, I am very glad to have had the opportunity to see that country at that time. It was an eye-opening experience that made us most appreciative of our United States, even with our problems. The tour was a personal view of history that I would never have had otherwise.

The management let the orchestra have a "stay-at-home" year in 1991 except for two Solti concerts at Carnegie Hall in New York, performances of the complete *Otello*, by Verdi.

Barenboim was now the music director of the Chicago Symphony, so the 1992 tour had him as conductor. We began with four concerts in the United States and then leaped across the Atlantic Ocean to Madrid. We had only visited Madrid one time before, on that cold January tour of 1985. Now we were able to get out and view the city. Of interest was the well-known museum of art, the Prado. It was fascinating to see, but unfortunately it had not been kept up well. The windows were dirty and gloomy. The lighting for the artwork was minimal. The paintings had been tainted over the years with grime and dust. Sometime later, attempts were made to clean the place, and to clean the oils too, but this often turned out to make them look phony, too new and glossy. I don't recall the final resolution of this problem, though the structure itself was much improved, we noticed, on subsequent tours.

On these trips, Paul Phillips and I strove to find the best eating establishments in each city, to indulge ourselves before going home to our diets. Many times Joyce Idema, the advertising manager of the orchestra, joined us. She was great in that position and usually had fascinating stories to tell about this artist or that conductor.

In Madrid we made arrangements to dine out. We knew that dinner had to be much later than in the U.S.A., as the Spanish have a long siesta in the afternoon each day and eat dinner quite late. We made reservations at a fine restaurant for 9:30 PM. We had the company of only one other table of diners. My, we were naïve. By 11:00 PM the place was filling up, and when we left at midnight the joint was starting to jump. Live and learn! We gave two concerts in Madrid and then two more in each of London, Cologne, and Paris.

Before we left Chicago for this tour, Paul and I made a dinner reservation at a famous Parisian restaurant, Lucas Carton, on the Place de Madeleine. It had elegant Art Deco décor, suave, worldly service, and great food. For a change of pace, the next night we were just out roaming around and came upon a café called Les Pieds du Cochon. Neither of us bothered to translate this name. We got a table, and in perusing the menu, suddenly realized that it means "Pigs' Feet." That is what they featured! Along with calf brains, and gullets of guinea fowl, and intestines of oxen. Oh dear, what had we done? They did have some shrimp dishes, perhaps for the tourists like us, so we indulged in that entrée. But the place was packed, so perhaps we are too prissy in America.

We were back home on April 17 for a short time. But on June 1 we left for Salzburg for a week's stay, doing the Whitsun Festival that is held every year seven weeks after Easter, on the holiday commemorating the descent of the Holy Ghost. We did this festival three times, which surprised us, as the Berlin Philharmonic had always done it before. Perhaps Von Karajan was busy elsewhere. Anyhow, Solti conducted two of the concerts and

Barenboim one. In addition, we recorded in the Festival Hall, with Solti, the Berlioz *Symphonie fantastique* and Liszt's *Les Preludes* on June 8. We were back in Chicago the next evening.

In 1993 we graced five cities in Florida, plus New York City for our standard two performances, before leaving for Salzburg on May 25 for the week of post–Easter Festival concerts. The tour continued in Spain; we went again to Madrid, but also to three new cities: Santiago, Valencia, and Barcelona.

What a disappointment was Valencia. After reading and hearing in the United States about this glamorous, enriching, enrapturing Spanish paradise, it was a shock to find it was nothing more than a manufacturing city. It was rife with smokestacks and river scows. At least we then went on to Barcelona, which we appreciated very much. We found it the most civil community that we had encountered in Spain. It has wide boulevards with a grand assortment of trees and flowers, in addition to many parks. The people are friendly and helpful. As you may have noted, I have not been too fond of Madrid, although it has some lovely areas. On all of our stops there, orchestra people had been mugged, women's purses grabbed from their arms, cameras and wallets stolen. This does not leave a good impression.

The next year rolled around; again it was May and we were off. We gave two concerts at Avery Fisher Hall in New York. We had only played there once before, a few years earlier, with Leonard Bernstein conducting. It was decided to try it again. This was the last time. The acoustics are simply not good, very dry and mushy. The New York Philharmonic must be constantly devastated when they realize that just a few blocks south is the fabulous Carnegie Hall. After a stop in Washington, D.C., we went on to our final year of the Salzburg Whitsun Festival, with three programs, followed by Frankfurt, Paris, London, and ending with a week in Cologne, where we gave four concerts, all of which were taped for TV. This was the first of our three engagements at the Festival Köln, which occurred in alternate years.

On each of these trips we had ten days or so in that city. We came to know it and like it. The Rhine River flows gently through the business area, alongside which is a lovely park, Rheingarten. A few blocks over is a plaza called the Alter Markt, Old Market, which has fine shops and interesting bars on the perimeter. This area had not been destroyed in the War's bombings. Up a small hill from this plaza is the famous Cologne Cathedral, which dates from the thirteenth century. It is a huge edifice. I like to believe that the cathedral was purposefully not struck with bombs during World War II, though some repairs had to be made.

Beyond this church is the main shopping area of the city. It had been severely damaged during the war and was rebuilt in that stark, now a bit dull, fashion of the '50s. But there are many fine shops and always charming salespeople. Adjacent to the cathedral is my favorite necktie center, Tina Farina. The ties are all hand-painted copies of modern artworks, or akin to such. Classy.

We found some new cities to visit on our May tour to Japan in 1995: Hamamatsu, Nigata, and Takamatsu, plus the usual of Osaka and five concerts in Tokyo. I gave a master class in Osaka for a group of flutists in their twenties. I tried to make the point that the notes and a lovely sound were just the beginning of music making. One has to play the emotion. If there is no story, as there is in an opera or a symphonic poem, then the player has to make one up to give the performance interest. If it is to be tragic, I suggested that they imagine they are in a café and have ordered sushi. When it comes to the table, IT HAS BEEN COOKED! Tragedy unbounded. After these remarks were translated, the audience broke up laughing. The flutist who was then playing actually did do a much better job of emoting. I guess she liked sushi.

The orchestra and Daniel Barenboim gave two Carnegie Hall concerts in November, both of which were concert performances of Richard Strauss's complete opera *Elektra*. This was a thrill for us, as were the many complete operas we did over the years with different conductors. I touch on this elsewhere.

On March 31, 1996, the orchestra left for Berlin for three concerts at the Berlin Festage (Festival). We had a full week in the city, as was often the case when we played more than one concert. This enabled us to get to know the cities, particularly on repeated trips. I had been to Berlin many times, starting on a holiday with a friend, Dr. John Clinger, in 1966.

John and I wanted to investigate Berlin and so took many long, out-of-the-way walks. We were amazed to see that just three blocks off the main streets the city was still in ruins. Rubble and parts of buildings were in evidence, and this was twenty years after the end of World War II. Also in view were bullet and shell marks on the sides of buildings which had not been blown up. Most of those marks have now been repaired and are not quite so noticeable.

We made our way to Friedrichstrasse and Checkpoint Charlie, then the gate into East Berlin and the return to West Berlin. For three blocks into East Berlin there was more rubble. The Russians did not want to repair it, as it now served as a buffer zone between East and West. After a few more blocks we came to the big main street, Unter den Linden. This had been a major section of pre-war Berlin, with the opera house, the concert hall, museums, cathedrals, and significant shopping. It was now heavily patrolled by Russian soldiers. The whole area had a devastated feeling, people almost slinking by on the streets. Turning right on the boulevard, we came to a plaza, called Lustgarten. At the far side was a large church, St. Matthew's. It was only a shell, the interior completely shattered. On another, later, trip we found that the inside had been reconstructed, unfortunately not in the old style of the exterior, but with a new, splashy look. There must have been a lot of history connected to it, as it became popular with tourists, so much so that in the late '90s they were charging admission to enter!

When we went past the Russian guards at Checkpoint Charlie we had to buy East German marks. I spent a few on some music at a shop, and John and I had a bit of lunch in a Bierhaus. Thank goodness he spoke German. In any case, we did not use all of our East German marks and we were *not* going to give them back to the Russians, as they would not exchange them when you left the area. We therefore tried to give them to some young people standing outside of the café. They were noticeably frightened. Finally, however, they understood that we were simple American tourists. They relaxed enough so that we could pass them our East German marks. They looked very grateful, but also got the heck out of there quickly—just in case, I guess.

Over the years I saw many changes take place in both Germanys, especially after the Berlin Wall came down. So in future years I did more exploring of the back streets. Staying at the Grand Hotel Esplanade was interesting, as it is in an area that is very close to what had been East Berlin. In fact, just across the street from the hotel is a small river, beyond which is a boulevard of large, pretentious buildings that had been embassies. In the war, they had been severely damaged and thus abandoned for years. I walked that devastated street many times, looking at what had been, now decayed, overgrown, and depressing. But it has been restored, though it is not an avenue of embassies any more.

Okay, on to touring! On September 4, 1996, we left for Birmingham, England. It is a charming city with a fine new hall. The acoustician Russell Johnson designed this hall, as he had done in Dallas and Lucerne. After two concerts we went to Dublin, our first time in Ireland, and then to Manchester and London, with two concerts, Solti doing Beethoven's Symphony no. 9 and Barenboim, Bruckner's Symphony no. 8.

In June we went to Cologne for three concerts at the Festival Köln. This began on June 2, 1997. On June 10 we visited Leipzig for the first time. At that period it was newly freed from the Eastern Bloc with the eradication of the Berlin Wall. The city looked sad and drab, as though it had been under a yoke. But the people were friendly and approachable and seemed to want contact and conversation. We played in a new hall, Gewandhaus, which was quite good, the old hall having been destroyed during the war.

A varied and interesting trip occurred in the fall of 1998, from August 30 to September 20. After two concerts in London and one in Birmingham, we flew to Brussels, where September is a lovely, warm time. Even more interesting is that it is the month for mussels. Each little café on the squares and small lanes had mussels with a different sauce. It was so pleasant sitting out in the open having mussels in Brussels!

From there we went to Baden-Baden, which is a spa city in southern Germany. The city had recently built a new concert hall that seemed to be quite good, except that it was painted, on the inside, all black. Rather grim. From there we hopped over to Lucerne for two concerts in three days.

The first chair players of the orchestra rotate off some of the music on the programs of a tour, both to rest and to let the assistant player have some repertoire. On this tour David McGill, the principal bassoon, and I withdrew from Beethoven's Symphony no. 7. In Lucerne that work was on the second half of one of the concerts, so we decided to eat at a gorgeous-looking Thai restaurant around the corner from the concert hall. The concert had started at 6:30. We arrived in the restaurant about 7:40. At 9 PM, while we were still at our table, conductor Daniel Barenboim and his entourage came into the room after the concert. He saw us at the table and with a sly little smile on his face came over to say hello. "I must tell you," he said, "that the Beethoven Seventh has never sounded better than tonight." We were shocked. And then we realized that he was slipping a gibe at us for taking off that performance. We all had a good laugh.

In earlier days while visiting Lucerne, I walked up the south side of the lake, Vierwaldstattersee. Along the shore is a house in which Richard Wagner and his wife Cosima lived when Wagner was in a mild exile from Germany. It was there that he wrote the *Siegfried* idyll. This is a short piece for sixteen instruments that he composed to celebrate Cosima's birthday. He gathered the players at the foot of the stairs. When Cosima came down in the morning the musicians played this work, based on themes from his opera *Siegfried*. I had played it many times and recorded it with Barenboim. It was a thrill to be in the area in which it had been written and first performed.

We were next in Munich, a very pleasant city. There is a wonderful art museum, behind which is a lovely city park through which I used to stroll, enjoying the scenery and the friendly people. The concert hall, Philharmonie am Gasteig, was fairly new. It did not have good acoustics at that time, having the same problems as the hall in San Francisco. It was much too open, with its ceiling too high and walls too far apart. The sound, therefore, was diffuse. San Francisco solved it, in part, by bringing in the walls, thereby losing 250 seats. Munich has made improvements too. They put reflectors in the ceiling to minimize the gaping space and to get the sound down into the audience's area.

We went on to Vienna for three days and two concerts. The main part of the city is built inside of a huge circle, around which is a grand boulevard called Ringstrasse. The Vienna State Opera is at one side of this ring. To the right of it is Karntnerstrasse. This was a main street at one time, with cars and public transport. However, sometime in the late '70s they blocked it off, covered over the road, adding plants and trees, and made it a mall for pedestrians only. It heads north for about ten blocks to the plaza of Saint Stephan's Cathedral. Just off to the left is another mall, called the Graben. That means "graves." Underneath this space are old catacombs from some medieval time. Spooky. Nevertheless, it is a busy shopping area.

After Vienna, the orchestra had a new experience. It's hard to believe that any new ones still existed, but they did. This one was Bucharest, Romania. The country was trying to recover from the despotic rule of the dictator Ceausescu, who had built himself a multi-million-dollar palace while the people were starving. Much to our surprise, the architecture of the city had a Spanish look about it.

Walking around the shopping area one day I noticed that the stores were empty. There were very few people on the streets. The place had a completely desolate atmosphere. Nevertheless, our hotel was quite wonderful. Hilton Hotels International had remodeled it. The dining room was actually fun, with a fine, exuberant staff. We had a waiter on several occasions who seemed to enjoy us too. He would try his few words of English and I would try my few words of French, which he spoke, and then we would all laugh up a storm. These are wonderful moments that allow great appreciation of people in a different land.

The first concert, at which we played Tchaikovsky's Sixth Symphony, was taped for television. The second concert featured Mahler's Fifth. We flew home the next day, September 20.

I had intended to leave the orchestra after the '97–'98 season, but Barenboim and the management asked me to stay another year to give them time to find a replacement. As a little nudge to me, they scheduled four performances of the Nielsen Flute Concerto, which we did in December 1998.

My last tour with the orchestra, then, took place in 1999, March 31 to April 4, with three concerts for the Berlin Festage. The Berlin hall, Philharmonie, has part of the audience seated behind the orchestra. There are several auditoriums like this now. The orchestra members never like them, and soloists up front do not either. This is because we all have learned to project our sounds out to the front. In fact, how does one project a tone to the back? Acousticians claim that the panels they install on the ceiling in front of the stage reflect the tone to the back. If so, it is a reflected sound, not the real tone that is being heard. Every time the current of sound is broken, a bit of the quality is lost. Of course, if an acoustician hears only volume and echo and not quality, he has no idea what a musician is talking about. As you might surmise, we have had unproductive experiences in attempting to communicate with acousticians.

My final three performances with the orchestra on tour gave me a bounty of pleasurable memories. Daniel Barenboim conducted the first Berlin concert. It was Brahms's *German Requiem*. We again had our Chicago Symphony Chorus to stun the audience; this was its first time in Germany. Our second program was led by Pierre Boulez, who did the Schoenberg opera *Moses und Aron* with a stellar cast and the great chorus. The final concert was an all-Strauss event: *Don Juan, Till Eulenspiegel,* and *Ein Heldenleben,* again with Barenboim. It was thrilling to me, and the audience felt likewise; the ovation proclaimed this. I think that Berlin was getting used to us and liking it.

The touring years of the Chicago Symphony Orchestra in which I was involved were 1958 through 1999. Looking back on that time, I am filled with overwhelming gratitude; the great number of cities we visited and revisited, the different concert halls we played in, the miles I covered while walking through these cities to familiarize myself with them, the unplanned experiences we adjusted to and appreciated, and the fabulous, different people we were privileged to meet. And of course, we mustn't forget the awesome amount of music that we played in all of those countries all over our planet. Also at the front of our memories is the astonishingly positive response we received from the audiences. It was a great place and time!

Have you noticed that in your life occasionally a coincidence occurs that is so extraordinary that it is almost not believable? If there is, perhaps, somebody "up there," I think that he must be impish, with a sly wit. In 1958 I played my *first* concert on tour with the Chicago Symphony Orchestra, in Boston. We performed *Ein Heldenleben*, by Richard Strauss. In 1999 I played my *last* concert on tour with the Chicago Symphony Orchestra, in Berlin. We played *Ein Heldenleben*, by Richard Strauss.

Forty-two years had passed and we were exactly where we started, musically. This coincidence of events made me feel that I had lived "A Hero's Life"! In addition, Boston begins with a B and Berlin begins with a B. How excitingly weird can it get?

4

"And how was the tour?"

A musician's diary of the European tour of the Chicago Symphony Orchestra, August to September 1981.

August 25, 1981, Tuesday, Chicago

Lufthansa flight LH431 left at 5:15 PM, non-stop to Frankfurt. The fourth European tour of the Chicago Symphony Orchestra had begun. It was a fine flight—a rather quick eight hours with good wine, a pleasant dinner, and an awful mess of a movie, *Eyewitness*. Half an hour's nap and suddenly it is 6:30 AM, achieved by setting clocks ahead seven hours. Breakfast, and arrival on time in a rainy Frankfurt.

August 26, Wednesday, Frankfurt

At the Hotel Intercontinental, I collapsed in bed for a long snooze after a 9 AM check-in. I had an early buffet dinner in the hotel and then took a long walk. What a renewal in Frankfurt since our first visit here in 1971! Then it looked shabby and dirty. Now they have refurbished the old buildings and covered the blighted areas with new attractive structures, including some dashing skyscrapers. There is a lush park through the central city about one block wide and at least a mile long, from the Main River to the Old Opera Plaza. Finding a small friendly bar near the hotel, I had two glasses of healthy German beer and dragged myself to bed at midnight.

August 27, Thursday, Frankfurt

Not a bad night's rest, considering my inner clock is seven hours off. A phone call at 10 AM woke me—a flutist from the Cologne Orchestra calling, hoping to get into a rehearsal of ours. All the concert tickets were sold out months ago, he tells me. After the inevitable continental breakfast I set out on a cathedral and antique shop tour of the old city: narrow streets with a medieval look. The rehearsal this afternoon was in a small hall, the Mozartsaal of the Alte Oper. Solti looked rested after six weeks' vacation and was raring to go. The Alte Oper was built in 1872 and gutted by the bombing in World War II. The façade is imposing in its Baroque splendor, but inside a completely new concert hall has been built, elegant and rich-looking with mahogany, crystal, and marble. The cost? $70,000,000!

August 28, Friday, Frankfurt

Awoke at 3 AM with Jet Lag Blues. I finally got up for real at 10. Then a walk to Palmen Garten, the Botanical Gardens of Frankfurt. I was amazed at the cleanliness of the streets and parks, with nary a piece of paper or cigarette butt to defile the walks. Lunch at the outdoor Opern Café on the plaza overlooking the Opera House. Rehearsal at 3 PM in the Mozartsaal. To bed early tonight, hoping not to wake up at 3 AM.

August 29, Saturday, Frankfurt

Rehearsal this morning in the main hall and concert tonight, Bartók's Concerto for orchestra and Bruckner's Fourth Symphony. Solti shaped a grand performance and the orchestra played beautifully. The acoustics of the new hall are ambiguous. It felt good to play on the stage, but reports from the audience say that the hall sounded too brilliant, almost raw, with no warmth or blend. A new hall usually needs some "tuning," so perhaps they will solve these acoustical bugs. We think that some ceiling panels, clouds, over the orchestra would help. That would give the orchestra good feedback, and blend the sound before it is thrown out into the hall proper.

Buffet wine and supper after the concert, given by the First National Bank of Chicago, and delicious it was. Solti was elated at the first concert of the tour and the audience response. All in all an auspicious opening for our tour, both concert and buffet.

August 30, Sunday, Salzburg

Same program as in Frankfurt, Bartók and Bruckner, but what a difference the Festival Hall made. This is certainly one of the greatest halls in the world. My choices for others are Carnegie Hall in New York and Gammage Auditorium, by Frank Lloyd Wright, in Phoenix. We notice that the best halls are normal theaters with a stage enclosure for the orchestra and a ceiling. Here the orchestra members hear each other, and themselves, so the sound is sent out to the audience adjusted and blended, rich, clean, and warm. We received a big reception from the audience, gratifying to Solti and to us in this hotbed of von Karajan—Berlin—Vienna.

August 31, Monday, Salzburg

Our second Salzburg concert and the closing of the 1981 festival was Beethoven's Eighth Symphony, Strauss's *Don Juan*, Barber's Essay no. 1, and Mussorgsky's *Pictures at an Exhibition*. Solti was in a broad mood tonight, so the *Pictures* seemed drawn out more than usual, but the audience loved it and applauded vociferously. For an encore we played the Scherzo from *A Midsummer Night's Dream* by Mendelssohn. It's a big flute piece, with lots of notes and tonguing, difficult at the end of a long concert. A glass of wine and a touch of food with friends, and then home (hotel) to bed. I'm quite tired. Will I never recover from jet lag?

September 1, Tuesday, Salzburg

A day off, and one week of the tour gone. I took a long walk through this quaint city, everybody's idea of "old Europe." There was a spectacular view from the top of the mountain behind the town. Directly below was the Festival Hall, pushed tight up against the face of the mountain. I enjoyed walking the paths through the trees, with bright-colored flowers still going strong, though the boxes of geraniums in absolutely every window get to be something of a cliché. A fifteenth-century defensive fort on a hilltop among the trees—how charming, we said. I wonder if people from the future will think that the atom bomb is charming. A very light supper tonight. Austrian food is just too heavy for me, with rich sauces, butter, potatoes, and bread. I have an unpleasant stomach upset, a rather common ailment on a tour. The reviews of the first Salzburg concert were raves. Paper #1: "Truly the greatest orchestra in the world—world-famous sound with no competition—great understanding of the music—a triumph." Paper #2: "Incomparable concert—the orchestral high point of the Salzburg Festival 1981."

September 2, Wednesday, Lucerne

Overcast and rainy, so the lovely lake and background mountains are obscured. The weather matched the mood of the orchestra when we checked in at the inferior hotels here, with rooms like cells, dingy and sparsely furnished. One of the non-joys of touring. The orchestra's complaints are heated. But in spite of it, and as always, the orchestra comes through at the concert for the Lucerne Festival, the Beethoven, Strauss, etc. But it is a loud, muddy hall, which will be replaced in a few years. We were not pleased but the audience was, thus, the Mendelssohn Scherzo for an encore again, with a fairly fast tempo, so the flute part "played" more easily. Back to my cell after a light Chinese supper with some orchestra friends.

September 3, Thursday, Lucerne

Decca/London Records gave us a two-hour boat ride on Lake Lucerne this afternoon with wine and snacks. It was pleasant except for the continuing overcast that prevented us from enjoying the views. Rehearsal this morning of the Mahler Ninth Symphony. It was barely more than a run-through, but tonight at the concert the orchestra did some wonderful playing and Solti conducted in top form. Wildly appreciative audience. The usual post-concert snack. The tour is now turning into a routine: eat, sightsee, eat, nap, practice, concert, eat, sleep—a bit too much eating in there. But I am determined that I *will* enjoy this tour!

September 4, Friday, London

Near disaster today—one of those negatively exciting elements of touring. The wardrobe and instruments left Lucerne early by plane but were delayed in London, first by fog, and then by recalcitrant customs officials. They finally arrived at Royal Albert Hall only a short time before the 7:30 PM concert was due to begin. The program was delayed fifteen minutes, but nerves were tense for longer than that. When the audience was informed that we would begin late they chorused one of their famous chants: "After waiting for three years [the last Chicago Symphony London performance was in 1978] what's another fifteen minutes?" A wonderful audience, six thousand strong and absolutely silent once the music starts. The *Don Juan, Pictures* program with the Mendelssohn encore went well, especially considering the long travel day for the orchestra of six hours, hotel to hotel.

September 5, Saturday, London

Arriving at Royal Albert Hall at 10 AM for a TV rehearsal, we saw scores of young people lined up outside. They had been there since dawn, waiting to buy standing room for our concert tonight. Dedicated! English flute maker Albert Cooper, who has revolutionized flute playing in the past ten years with his adjusted intonation scale and his new embouchure cut (the section of the flute into which you put the air), brought me a new silver head joint. It has a warm, big tone. I'm thrilled! We then had lunch and much flute talk at a quaint restaurant in Chelsea, La Popte, where I ate in 1976. Amazing how it looks much the same now. That's continuity. The concert tonight was one of the best. The Bartók Concerto for orchestra was taped for TV. We suffered a bit under the heat and brightness of the lights, but it went very well. The Bruckner Fourth after intermission showed Solti and the orchestra in peak condition. He conducted with less angularity and with more flexibility. It was a great performance. The sold-out audience went wild cheering. Had a late dinner with long-time English friends, a group of eight. I'm exhausted from the conversation—vibrant, intelligent, witty, and interesting. Happily to bed at 2:30 AM.

September 6, Sunday, London

Horrendous awakening at 8:12 AM with pneumatic drills doing their cacophonous ear damage outside the window. An emergency, they said. Not very sporting, I say. But it's a day off in London, with beautiful sun and warm air. I took a walk on quieter streets and in the parks, ending up at St. Paul's Cathedral. The bombs in World War II had destroyed many of the buildings around the cathedral, but St. Paul's was not touched. It was called "a miracle, divine intervention." Strange that when British and American bombers almost leveled Cologne, Germany, yet merely damaged the space around the spectacular Cologne Cathedral, we called it "pin-point bombing technique." I met flutist Kate Lukas later for a light dinner. We were aghast to realize that we couldn't have a glass of wine till 7:30. It was only 5 PM. Those strange hours of the English drinking laws; no service from 2 to 5 on weekdays and from 2 to 7:30 on Sunday! In most other ways the British are quite civilized.

September 7, Monday, Milan

Another six-hour travel day, hotel to hotel. Orchestra very tired, and annoyed, especially when we found on our arrival that all the restaurants were closed until 7:30. Our concert was at 8:30. We made a run on the fruit stand across the street from the hotel. The proprietor was astonished at the surge in business. The concert at La Scala was good but not great: Beethoven's Eighth, *Don Juan*, Bartók's Concerto for orchestra, and the Scherzo for an encore. The orchestra tried its best but we just couldn't overcome the travel fatigue, nor the dull, dry acoustics of the hall. La Scala may be great for opera, but not for concerts. We played out in front of the stage on a platform over the pit. Friends from Florida visiting Europe to buy a new Mercedes, and currently in Milan, met me for a post-concert dinner. It was wonderful, the best meal of the tour, at Café Don Lisander on Via Manzoni. We ate on the patio under the trees in the balmy air. Wow, such atmosphere!

September 8, Tuesday, Milan

I walked to Milan's center, forty minutes from the hotel, to meet my Mercedes friends for breakfast on La Scala Plaza. Then a bit of shopping. Milan has some lovely shops, many charming inner patios, the famous Galleria, that strange cathedral called Duomo, and La Scala Opera, but basically it is an industrial city—noisy, dirty, and frantic. Concert tonight, same program, sounded like a different orchestra. We were rested. The encore again was the Mendelssohn flute concerto, as Solti dubbed the Scherzo, and it was at its best, fast and bright. Dinner again at Café Don Lisander. With so much such delicious food and wine, I feel a diet coming on.

September 9, Wednesday, Bonn

This is the only city on the tour in which we haven't played before. The program was Beethoven's Eighth and Bruckner's Fourth. It took place in the Beethoven Halle, a modern concert hall with all that implies. The ceiling looked like the inside of an egg crate—rather intimidating. But the most memorable episode of the day took place after the concert. A party was given for the orchestra and various Bonn societies at the home of a Bonn gentleman of the government. He had redone an old railroad station into a wondrous mansion/art gallery. The main hall was all white and displayed his collection of modern art. Upstairs was a grand salon where the party for two hundred people was held. On the balcony of this room was a table the size of a Greyhound bus, for the sumptuous food buffet and champagne, wine, and beer. A spectacular setting and event.

September 10, Thursday, Vienna

We missed Vienna on the '78 tour, so it felt good to return now. The evening had no concert, but I heard several orchestra players practicing their instruments in the hotel as I did, just to keep the fingers and lips in shape. There is really no day off on tour. Decca/London Records gave a party in Unterdöbling to celebrate the new wine, Heurigen. I did not attend but I heard that it was not the food or the wine that made the evening, but the international opera star from Vienna, Lucia Popp, who acted as hostess. In a peasant costume, she helped to serve the meal, and then sang some Viennese folk songs with the performing string quartet. I went to Vienna's English Theatre to see Agatha Christie's *Murder at the Vicarage*. It had a full house and was a fun show, a light change from the past two weeks. Dinner afterward at one of my favorite restaurants in Vienna, Restaurant Rauchfangkehrer, corner of Weihburggasse and Rauhenstein, a block from St. Stephan's Square. It's been there for many years.

September 11, Friday, Vienna

A cloudy, grimy day off, but our mood was bright. These four nights in Vienna, in the same bed and situation, are heaven-sent, or Edwards-sent, to a tired orchestra. (John Edwards, general manager of the Chicago Symphony, who always seems to have the good of the orchestra at heart.) They will give us time to rest, take care of laundry, go gift shopping for The Folks Back Home and generally collect ourselves. From now on it is really rough, with seven concerts in eight days in six different countries. Tonight a friend and I went to the Vienna Opera to see Puccini's *Tosca* with Janis

Martin, Giorgio Merighi, and Eberhard Wächter. The Vienna Philharmonic was in the pit. The Philharmonic is actually the State Opera Orchestra and plays only a few symphony concerts each year. They sounded marvelous. There is no denying the appeal of the Vienna string sound, rich, warm, and glowing. The very blended brass adds impetus to the sound instead of overriding it. The winds and horns fill in the center with a mellow quality. Horst Stein conducted. I enjoyed it all, including the substantial and beautiful production. The Vienna State Opera Theatre, built in 1868, is not a blockbuster like the Paris Opera House. It is rather subdued; tasteful in cream, white, and gold with a muted velvet curtain in beige. It has wonderful acoustics. Both the singers and orchestra were heard well, with a natural warmth and clarity.

September 12, Saturday, Vienna

I went on a walking tour of the "Old City" this morning. I saw the house where Mozart composed *The Marriage of Figaro*, and the house where Beethoven wrote *Fidelio* and lived for twelve years. I also went into several old churches that were plain, even drab, on the outside, but inside they were a phantasmagoric Baroque display! Such a mish-mash of carvings, paintings, marble pillars, gilt trim, statues, geegaws, and stuff. It was not entirely unpleasant—it only made me slightly cross-eyed. Our first Vienna concert was tonight, Beethoven's Eighth and Bruckner's Fourth. The Musikverein Hall is small, only seating 1400, and very live. Because of this, the concert was much too loud. Dinner afterward at Café Dubrovnik, a favorite orchestra hangout in Vienna with spicy Slavic specialties. A trio of violin, piano, and bass played gypsy melodies with great gusto, to match the food.

September 13, Sunday, Vienna

It has been such a change to live and shop in Europe on this tour because, since the last tour, our dollar has dramatically climbed in relation to other currencies. On the '78 tour, we were suffering. Everything was so expensive. Now it seems no more so than at home, and in the case of a fine meal, it seems cheaper here. The second Musikverein concert had the same program as the first. I felt that Solti and the orchestra made some adjustments to the playing tonight, so the sound and the music making were more suited to this small auditorium.

September 14, Monday, Paris

Il pleure à Paris, but not inside the Théâtre Musical, where we played Mahler's Ninth Symphony to a packed house. All was sunshine as we gave a shining performance. An ovation followed. Conductor Daniel Barenboim, of L'Orchestre de Paris, attended our concert and came backstage to greet us. A late dinner then with a long-time Parisian friend at a "French-chic" café bar, with bizarre modern décor, yet elegant. It was noisy, dark, crowded, and immensely enjoyable. It was very French.

The orchestra is all chewed up! There are no screens on the windows at the Grand Hotel, and no air conditioning at this time of year. So the open windows to cool us invited in the hungry French mosquitoes. They thought we were part of foreign aid.

September 15, Tuesday, Brussels

A train ride today from Paris. I passed the time playing bridge in one of many such games. Concert tonight in the charming Palais de Beaux Arts, a mixed-bag program: Beethoven's Eighth, *Don Juan*, Barber's Essay, and Bartók's Concerto for orchestra, and yet another Scherzo encore. We have played here on all of our European tours and I always enjoy it. The hall gives the orchestra a beautiful tone, and it adds a touch of glamour and sheen to the sound of the individual players. It has us phrasing in a more spontaneous manner, and Solti is even more creative in his interpretation. Good acoustics do make a difference.

September 16, Wednesday, Amsterdam

Another train ride and more bridge. We haven't played here since the tour of 1974, so it was interesting to be back in the Concertgebouw, a famous hall. We did Mahler's Ninth Symphony. I must say the strings sounded positively luscious. The "live" acoustic was kind to them, though it was a bit difficult for us to hear each other clearly. Should I beat the drum again for some panels over the orchestra? A standing ovation!

September 17, Thursday, Amsterdam

A day off. I went for a stroll with friends in the city along the canals and the busy, finely stocked shopping areas. It is a dangerous experience to walk on the sidewalks here. One must do so *very* carefully. We want to urge the U.S. Congress in its next batch of foreign aid money to include two million guilders to Holland for pooper-scoopers! We had lunch at one of the many popular Indonesian restaurants, a meal called *rijsttafel*, "rice table." It consists of nineteen dishes of exotic flavor and variety, with rice on the side. It was delicious, as was the bottle of Blanc Bordeaux Sec '79.

September 18, Friday, Hamburg

Into Germany again—astonishing how clean, orderly, and alive the German cities look. The people seem directed, zesty, and socially responsible. Whatever happened to decaying London, grimy Brussels, Paris, Milan, and all the rest? Whatever happened to *us?* Concert in the Musikhalle followed by a dinner given by Teldec and Hines Cognac at a small restaurant on the waterfront. The menu was one of gourmet Richard Strauss's favorites: salmon and scallop tartare, chilled cucumber soup with caviar, filet de turbot on fresh spinach leaves with basis crème sauce and fresh garden herbs au gratin, and crêpes Jarnac, served with a 1979 Château La Berrière followed by Cognac Hines Antique. Returning to the hotel along the waterfront we saw Hamburg ladies of the night offering their wares. There was a traffic jam of shoppers.

September 19, Saturday, London

The final evening of the tour was in the Royal Festival Hall, Mahler's Ninth Symphony. It was a concert to remember. On a tour of outstanding performances, this was a worthy finale. How proud of us I am! After the concert, Amoco hosted a party on the roof of the hall. What a fiasco! Better to have done nothing than to have a few cans of Coke and beer set up on a table, with a couple of plates of small sandwiches. Not an appropriate ending to a musical evening of eloquence and a tour of greatness.

September 20, Sunday, London to Chicago

Sir Georg Solti and Lady Valerie gave the orchestra a brunch this morning in their large garden at their home in St. John's Wood. Inviting us into their residence was a most gracious gesture. The affair was friendly and informal. Then the buses to the airport and BA flight 298. Another ghastly movie—*Cannonball Run*. We arrived in Chicago on time at 4:45 PM. Glad to be home, but pleased about the tour with its fine music making of style and love. "And how was the tour?" we were asked. The best!

Above right: Mozart Concerto for flute and harp at Ravinia with Druzinsky and Ozawa, July 1971. *Peck collection.*

Below right: Peck, Druzinsky, and Reiner taking a bow after performing the Mozart Concerto for flute and harp, April 1963. *Rosenthal Archives, Chicago Symphony Orchestra.*

DONALD PECK

SOLOIST WITH

THE CHICAGO SYMPHONY ORCHESTRA

performing Gesenway's Concerto for Flute and Orchestra
Hans Schmidt-Isserstedt, Guest Conductor

ORCHESTRA HALL

Thursday, January 27 at 8:15 and Friday, January 28 at 2:00

Tickets $2.50 to $6.50 on sale at Orchestra Hall

Mail orders to: Orchestra Hall, 220 S. Michigan Ave., Chicago, Illinois 60604
Please include stamped, self-addressed envelope.
Phone information: 427-0362

Left: Gesensway concerto advertisement, January 1966.
Rosenthal Archives, Chicago Symphony Orchestra.

Above: Saint Basil's Cathedral, Red Square, Moscow, during
the Russian tour, November 1990. (Solti center, Peck right
of center.) *Rosenthal Archives, Chicago Symphony Orchestra.*

World premiere of Morton Gould's Flute Concerto, April 18, 1985.
Rosenthal Archives, Chicago Symphony Orchestra.

Peck, CSO manager Paul Chummers, the Duchess of Kent, and Lady Valerie
Solti in London, January 1985.*Rosenthal Archives, Chicago Symphony Orchestra.*

Donald Peck and friends—promo shot for December 4, 1988, concert (left to right: principal cellist John Sharp, principal bassist Joseph Guastafeste, Melody Lord, principal violist Charles Pikler, concertmaster Samuel Magad, Peck). *Rosenthal Archives, Chicago Symphony Orchestra.*

Peck performing the Nielsen Flute Concerto, December 17, 1998.
Rosenthal Archives, Chicago Symphony Orchestra.

Discussing Debussy's *Prelude to the Afternoon of a Faun* with Sir Georg Solti
in Salzburg, August 1978. *Rosenthal Archives, Chicago Symphony Orchestra.*

Peck at home, March 1985. (Wall photos, top left to right:
Fritz Reiner, John Browning, Daniel Barenboim, Erich Leinsdorf,
Sir Georg Solti and Peck; middle: Julius Baker, William Kincaid,
Eugene Ormandy, Rafael Kubelik, Eileen Farrell; bottom:
Lee Swinson, Louis Gesensway, Carlo Maria Giulini, Igor
Stravinsky, Jean Martinon.) *Kathleen Goll-Wilson, photographer.*

5

Guest Conductors

*T*he Chicago Symphony Orchestra had an extensive and impressive list of guest conductors, who took over for a few weeks each season when the music director was involved elsewhere. There was also an occasional unimpressive or downright unpleasant guest, who was usually not invited back unless we were unlucky.

One of the very good gentlemen was Pierre Monteux. He had been music director of the San Francisco Symphony for many years and then went to the Boston Symphony with a title akin to our "principal guest conductor." For many summers he had been a guest at the Ravinia Festival, summer home of the Chicago Symphony. That familiarity had bred respect, so we were very pleased when in January of 1961 he was to conduct us during our winter season at Orchestra Hall.

This was his last visit to Chicago. He had some trouble getting to the podium; walking was a problem for him. But, once there, he was as alert and keen as ever. His beat was clear but small and told us exactly what he wanted from the music. The orchestra responded with alacrity. In previous years he had recorded the Franck Symphony in d minor twice, but his recording company, RCA, decided that they wanted a new version with him. So he programmed this on his concerts with us. We then recorded it. Many people consider this to be the best recording of the Franck ever made. It was issued on LP at that time and was later transferred to CD. It is on the shelves to this day.

Sir Thomas Beecham came to the Chicago Symphony in his later years. At this time he was afflicted with gout and had a difficult time entering and leaving the stage. There was a stool on the podium, with a back, on which he sat to conduct. He used small gestures and gave the orchestra credit for knowing something, so we responded beautifully to him. He had a wry sense of humor and was sometimes a bit pungent, as at one concert when he was conducting "Brigg Fair," by Delius. He was enjoying it and sang along with the orchestra. There were a few coughs in the audience and suddenly Beecham stopped conducting, turned to the audience, and yelled, "Be quiet, be quiet! I can't hear myself sing." He then continued conducting. So that gave us an appreciation of his wit.

I give Beecham credit for changing the sound of English flute playing. Before World War II and after, English flutists did not use vibrato. They tended to sound like clarinets. During the war Sir Thomas came to the United States, where he became musical director of the Seattle Symphony, certainly a time of glory on the West Coast. After the war he went back to England with the sound of American flute players in his ear. In England at that time there was a marvelous flutist, Geoffrey Gilbert. He had studied abroad for a time and had acquired a vibrato, but still kept his deep, rich, full sound. He was having trouble getting a job in London because they were not used to vibrato on the flute. Beecham at this time was forming the Royal Philharmonic Orchestra. When he heard Gilbert play he knew that this was the flutist for him. He hired him.

Most of the English flutists who then followed studied with Geoffrey Gilbert, or with students of his, so this definitely established a new school of flute playing in England. It had an effect around the world, since many of these students became world travelers in music, such as James Galway, William Bennett, and Jacques Zoon. Thank you, Sir Thomas.

Leonard Bernstein had conducted the Chicago Symphony Orchestra at the Ravinia Festival in earlier years, before I joined it. He didn't return until much later, in 1988. He scheduled two weeks of programs, the first week with Shostakovich's Symphony no. 1, and the second week with Shostakovich's Symphony no. 7. We recorded both of these Shostakovich works with him for Deutsche Grammophon. The First Symphony recording is very good, but the Seventh Symphony is simply spectacular.

The Seventh is a very long work, with the first movement alone requiring thirty-one minutes. It is said to exemplify the fearsome invasion of Leningrad by the Nazis in September 1941. There is a short, trivial tune that begins very softly, and gradually over several repetitions builds to a grotesque climax, signifying the fall of Leningrad. Over the years, this movement had been cut here and there to shorten the performance a bit. Bernstein questioned the orchestra during a rehearsal, asking if we wanted to make some or all of the cuts, or play the movement complete. As a group we all yelled back, "Play it all!" So Lenny smiled, nodded, and that is what we did.

Bernstein had a bit of a complex about the Chicago Symphony because Fritz Reiner, who had shaped this orchestra, had been his teacher years ago at the Curtis Institute of Music. He seemed to have a touch of paranoia about that. Bernstein was slightly edgy with us in his first few days, but then he realized that we appreciated him, and Reiner was no longer on the scene. He relaxed and became warm and friendly. Unfortunately, he wanted to smoke all of the time. He became upset when management told him that he could not smoke on the stage. Every time one of us would walk off the stage, there he was, having a cigarette. In any case, at this time he was not a young man, and never returned after these two weeks. The orchestra was very happy, however, that we had had the experience of performing with him, and of making that wonderful Shostakovich Seventh Symphony recording.

I do have a more personal story about Leonard Bernstein which I always find amusing, that occurred a few years before he came to conduct us. A friend and I went out one evening to see a play. Afterward we stopped in a bar on the north side for a nightcap. Sitting across the bar area was Leonard Bernstein. He had ten drinks lined up in front of him.

A friend of ours, Ron, was in Bernstein's group and saw us across the room. He came over and told us that we had to meet "Lenny." He would introduce us. So we walked over to the area. Our friend spoke quietly with Bernstein, telling him that we were there to meet him. Ron suddenly turned red in the face. He told us, with embarrassment, that he couldn't introduce us because Bernstein didn't want anyone in the bar to know who he was. Now, really—did he think the customers in the bar had sent those ten drinks to him as a complete stranger?

Eugene Ormandy was the musical director of the Philadelphia Orchestra for over forty years. He came to guest conduct in Chicago during many seasons. He always brought his own string parts. These had the bowings for the string instrumentalists to utilize. Within ten minutes we were sounding like the Philadelphia Orchestra, which was noted for its spacious, emotional, rich sound. In earlier years Ormandy did not conduct with a baton. We had noticed over the years that the conductors who did not use a baton, like Stokowski and Ormandy, usually achieved a fuller, rounder tone from the orchestra. Giulini and Leinsdorf, both with mellow sounds, held a baton but usually left it hanging between the fingers and gestured with the hands and arms. This takes a bit more body action. Later, because of some health problems, Ormandy took to using a baton to minimize his motions.

The last time that he came he did Beethoven's Eighth and Ninth Symphonies. One of the first chair wind players, who had never been fond of Ormandy, turned to me after that concert and said, "Well, I've not always been happy with Ormandy, but this was the greatest Beethoven Ninth that I have ever played. I take back everything I have said before." I admired him for saying that, but I was also glad that he appreciated Ormandy finally, as I always had.

When my flute teacher, William Kincaid, retired as principal flutist of the Philadelphia Orchestra in the early '60s, Ormandy offered me the position. At that time I wanted very much to accept this offer, since I had studied in Philadelphia and had grown up musically with that orchestra. I was devastated when the Chicago orchestra management refused to release me from my contract. Such a refusal would not happen today, but at that time, managements were the tsars of the business. The musicians had no say, as I describe in the section on Jean Martinon in chapter 1, "Music Directors." In any case, the Philadelphia Orchestra waned a bit a few years later, after the hiring of Riccardo Muti as music director. At the same time the Chicago Symphony was hitting its world stride with Solti. Philadelphia as a city developed severe urban problems while Chicago maintained itself, and even grew in beauty, glamour, and artistry. So, if we just follow our fate, things do turn out just fine.

Another ex-Philadelphian who conducted in Chicago many times was Leopold Stokowski. He too had a sound of great beauty, maybe lighter than Ormandy's, but sweet and sensual. He arranged the orchestra in an unusual pattern, with the winds and brass on his right. To the left were the strings, with the basses across the back of the stage.

He first came to us in the fall of 1962, when Reiner was ill and could not open the season. Stokowski performed all of the music that Reiner had scheduled, music that was not necessarily associated with him. Nevertheless, Stokowski knew it all and put his own essence on it, which was always something special. Sometimes he was criticized for not being more academic, but at least he was always fascinating. He was a needed buffer against Arturo Toscanini and others, who pursued only a technical reflection of the printed page. Stokowski wanted the page played correctly and properly, but then he wanted to interpret what the music might be about, to infuse it with atmosphere.

We made many recordings with Stokowski on RCA, including the Shostakovich Symphony no. 6. This presented quite a challenge to me, since in the 1940s he had recorded it with the Philadelphia Orchestra and my teacher, William Kincaid, had played the extended flute solos in the first movement with absolute beauty. I am proud to say that I believe our recording is very, very good.

On one of his concerts in Chicago he began the program with his orchestration of Bach's Toccata and Fugue in d minor. The ending work was *Capriccio espagnol* by Rimsky-Korsakov. The *Capriccio* has cadenzas for several instruments, including the flute, violin, clarinet, and harp. We were told to make up our own cadenzas when the time came and not do the written ones. The idea came to me to tie the whole concert together by playing, in my cadenza, part of the main theme of the Bach Toccata from the beginning of the program. When I did this, Stokowski looked at me with amazement and gave me an appreciative grin. The players doing the other cadenzas followed suit and included some of the Bach in their cadenzas too.

Once, on a vacation trip to Oslo, Norway, my traveling friend, John, saw Stokowski in the lobby of the hotel. John told me to go over and say hello. I replied that I didn't want to bother him, as he wouldn't know who I was. But John went to greet him, and then Stokowski came over to me with a friendly smile. "Are you coming to my concert?" he asked. I said that we had tried to get tickets but that it was sold out. "Not for you," he announced. "I will call you later with tickets." And he did, and we went to the concert. I have always felt that I should have invited him out afterward for some food, or a drink. He could always have said no, but the gesture would have been made. I was too shy.

Glancing at what I have written above, I suddenly realized that the Chicago Symphony has recorded on CD almost all of the Shostakovich symphonies. We did 1 and 7 with Leonard Bernstein; 4 and 5 with André Previn; 6 and 10 with Leopold Stokowski; and 8, 10, 12, 13, 14, and 15 with Sir Georg Solti. That's a pretty good listing!

A noted conductor who appeared with us over the years was Erich Leinsdorf. He had been music director of the Rochester Philharmonic, the Cleveland Orchestra, and the Boston Symphony Orchestra. He worked very well in Chicago. I clearly remember a gripping production of Strauss's *Le bourgeois gentilhomme*, an exciting Frank Martin Concerto for seven winds, and his arrangement of a suite from the Debussy opera *Pelléas et Mélisande*. We heard stories of problems in Boston: overcontrolling of the orchestra's playing, and lack of agreement with the management on schedules, tours, and programming. This side of him was never manifest to us. However, we did see a part of him that was slyly wicked, or wickedly sly, as the next paragraph describes.

In 1960, we recorded Brahms's Piano Concerto no. 2 with Leinsdorf and a Russian pianist. In 1979 we recorded Brahms's Piano Concerto no. 1, again with Leinsdorf and another Russian pianist. Leinsdorf came to the podium for the second rehearsal of the First Concerto and said, "Now ladies and gentlemen, let us rehearse the Brahms concerto again." He abruptly stopped himself and said, "I don't know why I said 'again.'" We haven't had any Brahms yet." It was obvious that he didn't like the way the Russian pianist had played the Brahms at the first rehearsal. Leinsdorf practiced further naughtiness. At every rehearsal and concert, and at the recording sessions, he brought to the stage a small black box, about two by four inches. He stuck it onto the side of the piano near his podium. We had no idea what this was. Someone was finally brave enough to ask Leinsdorf about it. "Oh," he said, "that's a deodorizer. Russians never bathe." He felt secure in talking to us in this manner in English because the Russian didn't understand English. They had conversed in French.

A conductor who came to Chicago a few times as a guest was George Szell, music director at that time of the Cleveland Orchestra. We had the distinct impression that, with the departure of Fritz Reiner in 1962, Szell wanted to become the next music director of the Chicago Symphony. He was nervous when he was here, so things did not go well at the concerts. He made mistakes on the podium, which resulted in the orchestra's looking bad. There was a terrible episode during one performance of Beethoven's Sixth Symphony. Szell was most emphatic, stating, "Watch me, watch me! After the storm scene, I will make a cut-off before we go on." The concert came. He did *not* make the cut-off. Half of the orchestra did make a cut-off as he had admonished, and the other half didn't. It was a scramble.

During each of his three performances of Schumann's First Symphony there were problems in the last movement: he might conduct or not conduct, give entrance cues or not give them. All in all, that three-week period was rife with conductorial errors. Although he had done a fine job with the Cleveland Orchestra, conducting the CSO was not his métier. For us, he was too much of a pedant.

A major director with whom we had a good relationship was Charles Münch, then of the Boston Symphony Orchestra. He was a completely different musical creature than George Szell. Except to let the orchestra review the notes, Münch need not have rehearsed at all, since there was no set pattern to his interpretations. Each concert of the same music was entirely different from the previous one. It could be very exciting and sometimes disturbing.

He programmed Debussy's *Prelude to the Afternoon of a Faun* on two separate visits with our orchestra. This is a problematic work for the flutist, since it has many, many long phrases in which the player doesn't want to breathe so as not to interrupt the flow of the line. Okay, so we practice, and do it, but it's helpful if we learn in advance, say at a rehearsal, what the tempo will be, so we can plan our air intake. Münch, true to his form, would be slow, moderate, or fast, depending on his mood that day. Traumatic!

In one concert, at the summer Ravinia Festival, he stretched out the phrases for eternity. After all these years, I think that we are just now finishing the piece! When it did end, however, he was very pleased, and motioned for me to come up front and take a bow from the apron of the stage. When I got near to him, he grabbed me around the shoulders. He pushed me forward at an alarming speed to the extreme edge of the stage. I thought that I was going to fall over into the audience. Fortunately, he was hanging on to me. After my one quick bow, he turned me around and propelled me back to my flute chair. I guess that he liked to control the physical as well as the artistic.

The orchestra felt rewarded in having experienced the presence and musicianship of Carlos Kleiber for two weeks of two separate years. He was the son of the Austrian former conductor Erich Kleiber. Carlos had a distinctive personality, with singular observations of life and music, not wayward, but sometimes different from the mainstream. He was not arrogant, but he definitely wanted things his way.

Once he was recording a Beethoven symphony with the Vienna Philharmonic at the Sofiensaal in Vienna. During one of the movements he was not happy with the way that the session was going, so he called for an intermission and went to his dressing room. When it was time for the intermission to end, someone went to Kleiber's dressing room to bring him to the podium, but Kleiber was gone. The manager called the Imperial Hotel and was told that Carlos had checked out and was driving back to Munich, where he lived. I don't know if they ever finished that recording.

We felt lucky to have had his visits to Chicago, since he rarely conducted outside of Europe, and in fact, very little there. We were the only orchestra in the United States that he ever directed, though he did do a couple of opera dates at the Metropolitan Opera and in San Francisco. His conducting technique was not time-beating. He molded the phrases in a musical fashion. The orchestra generally liked him very much, except for the few who were more technically oriented. One time, during a rehearsal of Brahms's Second Symphony, one of the first chair players raised his hand. "Maestro," he said, "can you beat clearer at letter D?" There was a gasp from the orchestra at this effrontery. Kleiber stood there looking at the player for quite a long time, and finally said one word: "No." There was a surreptitious shuffling of feet by the other members of the orchestra in appreciation of Kleiber.

Whatever his idiosyncrasies, he did present exciting, thought-provoking concerts. We were sorry when he canceled his third season with us and never returned. He went to live on a mountain slope outside Munich and did almost no conducting. He died in 2004, to the world's loss. He was buried in Konjsica, Slovenia, next to his ballerina wife.

In the early '60s, the CSO podium was graced by a gentleman of high sensitivity, Hans Rosbaud, conductor of the Southwest German Radio Orchestra. He was no longer a young man and not famous. World War II had hampered his career. He came to Chicago many times, always giving great music to the audience and to the orchestra. Off the stage he was a sweet man, interested in conversing in a quiet, friendly manner. The last concert that he ever conducted in his life was given with the CSO in December of 1963. It was Mahler's Symphony no. 9. He knew that his days were few. During the third performance of the Mahler he wept while leading us. Back home in Germany in January, he died. We heard that it was cancer. We thank the powers that be for making this gentleman available to us.

Two American conductors worked with us on occasion, Michael Tilson Thomas and Leonard Slatkin. They were both knowledgeable, but they had entirely different approaches to music, and to the world.

Slatkin was a quiet person who treated the orchestra in a gentlemanly fashion. At rehearsals he made his wishes known in a clear, easy manner. He was never out to bolster his image with physical displays, but only wanted to make beautiful music, which he did. Since he did not gesticulate violently, as do many directors, some members of the audience did not feel that he was "getting into it." I say, music is to be heard, not to be looked at.

One year he did the music to Ravel's complete ballet, *Mother Goose*. It appeared to a few that it was underplayed. However, listening to the broadcast of that concert a few weeks later, I was entranced with the spacious beauty of the performance, completely natural and unmannered. In another year I played a solo with him, the Telemann Suite in a minor for flute and strings. I had performed this work many times. This was absolutely the best. He was very sensitive to my approach at the three concerts. His directorship of the St. Louis Symphony brought it to a fine peak. After twenty years he left, to take over the National Symphony Orchestra in Washington, D.C., a position he gave up in 2005.

Michael Tilson Thomas was another story. His rehearsals were uninteresting and much too long, since he appeared to consider them a time for oration. We felt that he should have been on stage in a Shakespeare play. We wanted to rehearse the music and get the heck out of there! The orchestra became bored, and the concerts reflected this. Nevertheless, he has found the right place for himself, as leader of the San Francisco Symphony. To them he seemed to be vital and full of life, as they had formerly been playing under Herbert Blomstedt, a fine technical man, but somewhat listless musically. Thomas's arrival was a blossoming change. He is doing very well there, and the city does suit his lifestyle.

Outstanding composers were invited to conduct the Chicago Symphony, with at least part of the program being music from their own pens. They were not always superior stick technicians, but it was a thrill to be performing the composer's music under his direction.

In my early days in the orchestra we were graced with the presence of Sir William Walton at the Ravinia Festival. He was every bit as gracious as the British always claim to be, with the usual wily sense of humor. His conducting was not bad either. He had experience, obviously. He did two concerts of his music, which included the Symphony no. 1, the Violin Concerto, the Viola Concerto, and the *Johannesburg Festival Overture*.

Igor Stravinsky came at least three times during my tenure in the orchestra, twice in the downtown winter season and once during the summer. I had played for him a few years earlier at the Santa Fe Opera, doing *The Rake's Progress*. He announced a whole series of recordings that he wanted to make with the CSO for Columbia Records, and that is where a problem surfaced.

In July 1964 we recorded two ballets with him, *Orpheus* and *Apollo*. The sessions went so smoothly that Columbia wanted to add another work on that day. The union and orchestra committee said no, that once the music for a session was announced, nothing could be added. This was at a confrontational period in the orchestra's history, involving the management, the musicians' union, and the players. Columbia Records was angry at the response and canceled all further recording with Stravinsky and the Chicago Symphony. I felt bad about this, as one of Stravinsky's works that had been scheduled for us in the near future was *Le baiser de la fée*. It has a huge flute part, with cadenza and all. He went to Cleveland and recorded it. We won our point, but lost the war. That union ruling was soon dropped. At least I had recorded that suite from the ballet a few years earlier with Fritz Reiner.

The American composer Lukas Foss was quite a good conductor and visited us a few times. At that time he was the musical director of the Brooklyn Philharmonic. He always scheduled some of his own works, and played the piano on occasion. One year we did the Bach Brandenburg Concerto no. 5 for piano, violin, and flute, with Lukas at the piano. On the same program I played a new flute and orchestra piece he had just finished called "Elytres."

Another appealing British composer with whom we worked was Sir Michael Tippett, who conducted us in March of 1974. In Tippett's concert, he conducted his Concerto for piano and orchestra and his Symphony no. 3. A few years later, in 1977, he wrote his Symphony no. 4 for Solti and the CSO, which we performed in London on one of our tours and also recorded. There were many composers over the years, including Gunther Schuller, Bruno Maderna, Paul Hindemith, and others. I would like to discuss two well-known Americans.

Aaron Copland arrived at the Ravinia Festival in July of 1968. On the podium he was always bouncy and perky, even in the soft, sensitive sections; I mean, what was he trying to do? We gave an all-American music program in the midst of a ferocious thunder and lightning storm. It was a long program: Barber's overture to the *School for Scandal*, Ives's "Decoration Day," William Warfield singing Aaron Copland's *Old American Songs*, and then the *Dance* symphony, Roy Harris's Symphony no. 3, and in the middle of all of that, Griffes's Poem for flute and orchestra. Why had Copland programmed the Griffes? He didn't seem to know it. I can't believe that he had ever even heard the work. I pulled together my so-called professionalism and did what I could. Strangely enough, I got two fabulous newspaper reviews, one of them saying, "I still find remarkable Peck's matchless control, sensitivity, and downright sensual interpretation." Maybe more conductors *shouldn't* study the score.

One American who has a significant history with the CSO is Morton Gould. In the 1960s, when Jean Martinon arrived as music director, the orchestra had a large recording contract with RCA. Martinon was not yet well known, so RCA wanted to spread out the taping sessions among some other conductors. One of those chosen was Morton Gould. We did a lot of recording with him: Rimsky-Korsakov, Miaskovsky, Copland, Ives, Tchaikovsky, and Gould's own work.

His knowledge of the music and friendly attitude made him much liked by the orchestra. He was a very talented composer, but had an unfortunate success in his early days. He had written, on request, a short piece called

The American Salute. It became a very popular work, played by every type of ensemble over and over. It gave a "popular" slant to Gould's reputation, which at times interfered with his "serious" reputation. I had an occasional lunch with him. He was always very pleasant. I found him to be a brilliant musician. It was because of this that I asked him to write a flute concerto for me in the '80s when money came as a gift from a donor. I will tell this story later.

We look back on a group of top conductors that we appreciated: Bernard Haitink, André Cluytens, Rafael Kubelik, Riccardo Chailly, William Steinberg, Paul Kletzki, Hans Schmidt-Isserstedt, Klaus Tenndstedt, and others. The middle group would include Kurt Masur, Loren Maazel, Zubin Mehta, Sir Andrew Davis, Joseph Krips, André Previn, Neeme Järvi, and Christian Thielemann. There were a few others that we never wanted to see again, although management occasionally would invite one back. They may have been acceptable with some orchestras, but the chemistry did not work with the Chicago Symphony.

One such was Günter Wand, from Hamburg, Germany. Although he might not have been so, he seemed very unhappy to be in Chicago and certainly unappreciative of us. We recorded with him, on his first visit, the Brahms Symphony no. 1. His approach to the music was studied, technical, and uninspired. When he came a second time, doing a Bruckner symphony, the orchestra and management were so offended by his rude behavior that a booked third season was canceled.

Another non-gentleman, who acted like a student of Wand's, was Michael Gielen. All of the above remarks apply to him as well. This man was a puzzle, since he was an assistant to Daniel Barenboim at the Staatsoper in Berlin. Barenboim sometimes ignores the technical side of conducting to bring out the musical aura. Gielen was exactly the opposite, too technical with no music. Unfortunately, "Danny" brought him back several times.

Riccardo Muti appeared with us a few times. At that time, he was distinctly the wrong influence for the CSO: driven, tight, and edgy. When he had a position with the Philadelphia Orchestra, he purposefully set out to change its famous sound. In so doing he ruined the essence of that orchestra. It wasn't until a few years later, with Wolfgang Sawallisch, that the Philadelphia Orchestra was able to regain some of its grandeur. Muti's attitude created problems at La Scala in Milan, where he was artistic manager, and eventually he left.

There is no need to dwell on the negatives, like Jakov Kreizberg, Fernando Previtali, and many others. To us they seemed egocentric, with no real musical ideas. But they may have found a niche for themselves elsewhere.

Every orchestra has its personality, as does every conductor, and sometimes they just don't mesh. The problem may be the attitude of the individual, but usually it is his approach to music making. If a negative conductor is on the premises for a week or so we can tolerate him, but we definitely look forward to the time when he will no longer be around, as perhaps the gentleman in question does as well. Our down feelings about some directors led us to admire even more the conductors that did fit with us as guests. Those that were engaged as contract members of the "team" are elaborated on in other chapters.

6

Learning a New Language; or,
The Sayings of the Conductors

*T*he orchestra played under many conductors who were foreign-born. Some of them spoke impeccable English, like Carlos Kleiber, Christian Thielemann, and Franz Welser-Möst. Others had a limited knowledge of the language or spoke with a heavy accent, sometimes on purpose, thinking that it made them appear glamorous. Both approaches often led to amusing or incomprehensible phrases. But a good laugh does relieve tension. Following are some of the conductor utterances that I wrote down over the years (my translations are in parentheses).

Sir Georg Solti

Solti did not try to confuse us, or be glamorous with an accent. It just happened that he spoke many languages and got his accents or grammar confused once in a while. So, some of his comments:

I need a few help (brass softer on long notes). 1992
I vant the tragic intonation (a sad quality). 1989
Swim into that between (instructions to clarinets in a new Tippet song cycle).
My dear everybody (his oft-used greeting). 1988
Cut off the moment it sounds like a lame duck. 1992
Did you been confused? 1984
Loud, but not scratchioso. 1995

I will faster as I was. 1989

Softer your noise passion (it's too loud). 1983

Don't over scratch (strings). 1990

Some desperado came in too soon. 1996

It's not that you're behind, it's that everybody's behind everybody (it's not together). 1992

1, 2, 3, 4—the fits bar (the fifth bar). 1987

You are stucking out in the fortepiano (the fortepiano attack is not together). 1988

I pested you for missing (please play with the beat). 1970

We need a little pesting (we must do that again). 1989

I don't pest you further (it's fine—we'll leave it). 1988

(Telling the strings how to bow a phrase) Dampen it with your butt. 1988

I forgotted to tell you. 1989

Did I broke it? (His glasses, which he had dropped). 1990

No Chinese intonation! (It was out of tune in *Das Rheingold*). 1983

Make a wonderful spookiness (in Mahler's Fourth). 1983

Let's have a Nazi concentration camp sound (make it more ferocious). 1990

When you don't play, it's pianissimo (softer). 1983

Old pensioner's semi-quavers (sixteenth notes are too long). 1982

That's a tired Monday-morning sound (too dull).

A little less super-Hungarian, please (Bartók's Concerto for orchestra). 1990

No democratic thirty-twos, please (you weren't together). 1984

Let me have that lovely two-flute crotch (he meant "crotchet"). 1987

Cut off the notes except for the last two—stay onish (?) 1987

We had a bit of a mish-shap (he meant "mishap"). 1989

No holiday vibrato (the vibrato was too slow). 1977

I hear a fish. (He meant a clam. Someone had played a wrong note).

I don't hear a sausage! (Solti often used this phrase. We didn't know exactly what he meant in the early days; then we realized that he wanted something louder. While on tour in Budapest one year I had dinner with the first flute and oboe of the Budapest Philharmonic. Since Solti was also Hungarian, I thought that these players would be able to tell me what "sausage" meant in Hungarian. They said that there was no word in Hungarian that sounded like that. They were as mystified as us. We finally decided that he must have had a word in mind meaning "louder," and mispronounced it so it sounded like "sausage." Ergo, we played louder.)

Erich Leinsdorf

The spirit of the ensemble is not necessarily preserved by body heat (there's no need to move around so much when you play. Said to a soloist). 1992

Too much tension. Make it pre-Freudian phrasing (without so much expression). 1989

It's blotter-paper pianissimo (it's too dull). 1989

The beginning isn't quite organic in the movement. (?) 1990

The details are all composed, so we don't need them. (??) 1990

When one plays shortissimo or shortello, we have a salami. (???) 1992

I don't want to become obnoxious, which is easy for me. (We laughed at this one). 1992

Daniel Barenboim

At a rehearsal, the trombones arrived late on the stage for their entrance in the fourth movement of a symphony. While waiting for them, Barenboim quipped, "Oh, that's all right. If they had been here it just would have been too loud." 1989

After a player had made an incorrect entrance: "If you don't know when to play, come in softer." 1993

André Previn

Previn was with us several times. One year we recorded two Shostakovich symphonies with him, numbers 4 and 5. He was knowledgeable, with a clean baton technique. The concerts were very well played, with control but leniency from the podium. At rehearsal he was calm and relaxed, somewhat like Leonard Slatkin.

One year we were rehearsing a Russian composition new to us. Previn said that we would play it through to get the idea of it. When we finished, Previn praised us. "That was wonderful! I have never heard an orchestra play a work so perfectly the first time. Now, let's try it again, and this time I'd like to hear a few wrong notes!" Well, you can imagine—we all played *many* wrong notes just to assuage him. He laughed each time.

7

Nights at the Opera

I was amazed at the large number of operas performed by the Chicago Symphony Orchestra between 1957 and 1999. In discussing this with the knowledgeable and affable Frank Villella, manager of the symphony's Rosenthal Archives, I realized that in retrospect it made perfect sense. Most of the conductors attached to the orchestra were current or past opera directors.

Fritz Reiner was at the Metropolitan Opera throughout his career, even conducting there at the time of his death. Sir Georg Solti was once on the staff of the Munich Opera, then moved on to head the Frankfurt State Opera, before becoming music director of the Royal Opera House in London. Furthermore, he had been at the Metropolitan, Vienna, and Chicago companies, to name a few others. Claudio Abbado had conducted at La Scala in Milan, as had Carlo Maria Giulini. Daniel Barenboim was major-domo at the Staatskapelle Opera in Berlin.

The opera performed most often by the Chicago Symphony Orchestra was Bartók's *Bluebeard's Castle:* fourteen performances and a recording conducted by Pierre Boulez with Jesse Norman as soprano. Beethoven's *Fidelio* we did in four separate years; we recorded it with Solti, then performed it with Eschenbach and Barenboim, making a total of eleven performances. At number three are Schoenberg's *Erwartung* and *Moses und Aron,* with Solti and Boulez, each done nine times. Coming in with six were Mozart's *Così fan tutte* and Verdi's *Otello,* with a Solti recording. We had five performances of Strauss's *Elektra* and four of *Don Giovanni,* by Mozart. We also performed single acts from all the Wagner operas with Barenboim, Levine, and Solti, with whom we recorded the complete *Fliegende Holländer* and *Die Meistersinger von Nürnberg* for Decca-London, as well as performing the full *Das Rheingold* at eight concerts over two different years.

The operas were given as concerts with no staging at Orchestra Hall in Chicago, often with a repeat at Carnegie Hall in New York. The singers stood in front of or amidst the orchestra. It was interesting and sometimes pleasantly amusing to see how different singers would react to this "stationary opera." Some just stood there and sang. A second group did some minimal gestures concerning the role. The third set could not forget how they usually acted the part on the opera house stage and found it difficult to suppress bodily movements or facial gestures. This was a completely understandable action on the part of the singers, but it was disturbing to the audience and the orchestra, since these were not staged presentations. Solti and Levine would sometimes make cautionary hand gestures to this group, saying, in effect, "Cool it, folks."

One of our favorite singers was Birgit Nilsson, who had a huge, clear, dramatic soprano voice. She sang with us many times, usually doing Wagner or Strauss. We loved her as a vocalist and as a charming person. She did some roles other than the heavy Germanic repertoire. I heard her in Puccini's *Turandot* in the Metropolitan production. She blew the house down, as the saying goes. She was also noted for some of the heavier Verdian heroines.

Her high register may have been favored. It was very full and easily produced, with never a tentative hint. She was most successful in that range. Her bottom register was considered to be a shade on the weak side. She never attempted to pump it out down low, as do some sopranos, who perhaps thereby taint their higher octaves. Nilsson possibly expanded or saved her fabulous high register through this caution. After all, she was singing soprano roles, and we wanted to hear her ringing high tones. She had recorded *Salome* in Vienna, with Solti conducting, so in 1974 he brought her to Chicago, where we did two performances, and then to New York for a third. Over the years she came to us with many Wagner excerpts, equally thrilling. Nilsson died on Christmas Day, 2005, in Sweden. She was eighty-seven years old.

At one point the orchestra management decided to try a semi-staging device when presenting an opera concert. This consisted of a large platform built over a quarter of the orchestra at the back of the stage. A staircase on both sides gave the singers access to the space. It was, in effect, a small opera stage. The singers reacted to each other during the arias and then sat at the rear of the platform when they were finished, as though they were off-stage. It worked very well. One of the first productions to use it was Berg's *Wozzeck*, in 1984, with conductor Claudio Abbado.

Wozzeck is one of the greatest operas of the twentieth century, with its heart-wrenching story and Berg's musical realization of it. Leopold Stokowski, at the American premiere he conducted in 1931, stated, "Berg has written the opera that was expected of his master, Schoenberg." A comment from Erich Leinsdorf says, "The vocal style is wholly in keeping with the demands of the drama, nothing stilted or artificial." Herbert von Karajan felt that it was one of the most devastating compositions to conduct. "It takes up all of your mind and heart. You will need two or three years to recover!"

Abbado did an exemplary job in Chicago, drawing in the orchestra, soloists, and audience. I mentioned in chapter 2 the fear the orchestra had when Abbado did the whole opera from memory. Another little issue did arise. Toward the end of act 1, a marching band parades by. In line with the semi-staging, Abbado wanted the management to hire an outside group of musicians to march down the center aisle of Orchestra Hall playing the band tune, and then up the stairs past the singers. His scheme didn't appeal to the management, as this would have required paying twenty or more extra players. The refusal outraged Abbado. He threatened to walk out of the whole production. We heard that there were many talks over dinners, with famous Italian wines and liqueurs, of course. Signor Abbado capitulated. He agreed that the orchestra winds could play the band music, seated on the stage.

Came the first rehearsal. During that section one of our sly trumpet players said to Abbado, "Maestro. How much are *we* to be paid for playing this extra music?" Fortunately, the whole orchestra broke up laughing, which indicated to Abbado that the remark had been a friendly joke. In any case, the three performances were thrilling. But, no extra pay.

Most of the opera presentations after *Wozzeck* made use of the raised platform at the back of the stage. These included Solti's *Moses und Aron*, May 1984; Abbado's *Boris Godunov*, November 1984; and Barenboim's act 2 of *Tristan und Isolde*, in November of 1985. (Some stories of these concerts are in another chapter.) We were surprised in 1991, when Solti was conducting *Otello*, to see that the singers were using a space cleared in the center of the stage, near the front. We learned that Decca-London was recording it live, and the sound was more to their liking in this staging. The same layout was used in September of 1995, when Solti and the orchestra performed the Wagner opera *Die Meistersinger von Nürnberg*, which was also recorded live.

In March of 1995, Barenboim conducted Strauss's *Elektra* using the raised platform. It is one of my favorite operas, and this performance certainly maintained my love. Starring were Deborah Polaski and Alessandra Marc. We had done it in 1986 at the Ravinia Festival, James Levine conducting, with sopranos Ute Vinzing and Leonie Rysanek. But by the time 1995 rolled around, 1986 was only a dim memory. I didn't recall the extremely difficult flute part to this opera. It has thousands of notes, in all keys, running rampant over the instrument. I was determined to play them all, and in the right place. Did I practice? You bet I did!

When the concerts came, I concentrated like crazy and did my best, which I must say wasn't bad at all. It was exciting just to be able to play the part, even leaving aside the musical side of it. So, in 2002, a friend and I flew to New York to see and hear *Elektra* at the Metropolitan Opera. James Levine conducted, with the marvelous sopranos Gabriele Schnaut and Deborah Voigt. It was one of those days of perfection, a great performance!

I was interested to hear the Met. Orchestra, as my mind had the memory of *that* flute part. I listened attentively, even with some knowledge of what I should be hearing. Well, to quote Sir Georg Solti, "I didn't hear a sausage." The orchestration is rather thick, and though I am sure that the flutists were playing all of those notes, they could have gone home and we wouldn't have missed a thing, except for a soft solo now and then. When I think of all the time I spent practicing that music—and for what? Nevertheless, I did have my pride in having accomplished it, even if no one heard it, although the rest of the flute section must have, and maybe even the oboes and clarinets. That's life in the orchestra sometimes.

The Ravinia Festival had tried the semi-staged opera as long ago as 1978. James Levine, who was the music director then, opted to conduct the mammoth Berlioz opus *Les Troyens*. Because of the length of each of the two acts, he presented one the first night, and the other on the second night.

The orchestra was placed on the ground level of the auditorium, as if it were an orchestra pit at an opera house. The front of the stage was "home" to the singers; the back part held the large chorus needed for this opera. A few props were positioned in the singers' area to allow for some acting and logical movement. The original cast assembled was to have been headed by Régine Crespin, but upon her cancellation, Shirley Verrett was hired. Although I was sorry we did not have Crespin, Shirley Verrett gave a magnificent performance as both Dido and Cassandra. Other singers of high quality were Claudine Carlson, Guy Chauvet, John Cheek, and Kathleen Battle.

The performance was wonderful, as all of the newspapers agreed the next day. And nature added her bit with a spectacular summer storm of thunder and lightning, definitely contributing to the Royal Hunt and Storm scene. The wags in the orchestra commented that since this was a French opera, Berlioz, up in the heavens, ordered the storm to give the impression of Paris, where it rains all of the time!

In his years at Ravinia Levine presented sixteen operas, often with more than one performance of each. One of the most successful was Mozart's *Don Giovanni* in 1988. It had a great cast, headed by Thomas Hampson as the Don; he was commanding, both vocally and physically.

We performed it again under Daniel Barenboim, who, in 1992, presided over a Mozart festival in Orchestra Hall, doing the three Mozart operas with libretti by Lorenzo da Ponte: *Don Giovanni, The Marriage of Figaro,* and *Così fan tutte.* For these concerts Orchestra Hall was transformed into a makeshift opera theater. The orchestra occupied a position at the front edge of the stage. Paul Steinberg and Christopher Alden then designed a raked platform, forty by nineteen feet, above the heads of the musicians, which supported the action of all three operas. It had white tilted walls framing a baroque room, complete with gold-backed chairs and candelabras. There were slight variations to accommodate each opera. The costumes were by Oscar de la Renta and Gabriel Berry, mixing some modern-day attire with eighteenth-century finery, especially for the female roles. Over a two-week period there were three performances of each opera on alternate days. The same cast members sang in all three operas. These included Cecilia Bartoli, Joan Rodgers, Waltrud Meier, Sheri Greenawald, Ferruccio Furlanetto, and Michele Pertusi.

This project had been planned some years before 1992. It was expected to cost $900,000, which was to be covered by extra donors. Unfortunately, no one planned for the recession that occurred at that time. Nevertheless, there never was any question of the orchestra's not honoring its obligation. According to Henry Fogel, CSO executive director at that time, "The Chicago Symphony did not get where it is by breaking promises. I'm very excited about the project."

The show did go on and was a huge success with the sold-out audiences and the press. The deficit problem was solved and the pride of the city and the orchestra soared to a high degree.

For those of us who like statistics, during my years in the Chicago Symphony Orchestra, 1957 through 1999, we performed forty-three different operas. With repetitions of most of them, this came to 160 performances, of which Solti conducted the most, with fifty-seven, followed by Barenboim, twenty-four; Levine, nineteen; and Abbado, twelve. Various other conductors each had one or two performances. We symphony musicians in Chicago felt pleased and privileged that we had been a part of so many operas, sometimes even staged. What a thrill to have worked with this array of glorious singers, as well as enjoying the change of musical genre from the regular symphonic repertoire.

8

Singers

*W*ith so many vocal performances and operas appearing on the schedule of the Chicago Symphony, the musicians were able to glimpse the backstage attitudes and onstage machinations of a host of famous singers, as well as their achievements.

My favorite singer when I was a boy was the American soprano Eileen Farrell. At that time I had three recordings of her singing Wagner that I played over and over. With Leopold Stokowski conducting, she did the *Wesendonck Lieder*. With Leinsdorf it was act 3, scene 3 of *Siegfried*, and, led by Charles Münch, the Immolation scene from *Die Götterdämmerung*. Farrell had a huge voice that was not forced. It effortlessly floated into the hall and filled it with a rich, sensual quality. In later years and at separate concerts, she sang those three Wagner selections with our orchestra at the Ravinia Festival, conducted by James Levine. Having lived my youth with the recordings, I was thrilled to be actually performing them with Eileen Farrell.

I went backstage to tell her of my admiration for her singing. She responded that she had been listening to the orchestra and was astonished that I had such a big flute tone when I had such a slim body. I answered, "But Miss Farrell, you have a huge voice!" Eileen Farrell always had a quick retort. She looked at me slyly and answered, "Yes, but I am as wide as you are tall." I think she overstated it just a bit.

One year she was appearing as soloist at a winter concert at Orchestra Hall, directed by Jean Martinon, performing the Immolation scene. At rehearsals singers often do not sing out full voice; they are saving it for the actual concert. This is called "marking." At that time the orchestra had a new, young cellist who didn't understand what marking was. He heard a lot of praise of Farrell, so when, at the rehearsal, she was marking and didn't sound like what he expected, he turned to his stand partner and said, "So, what's so great about Eileen Farrell?" Nevertheless, at the concert that evening Eileen Farrell *was* Eileen Farrell and let out that grand voice that filled the hall. The cellist, while moving his bow across the cello strings, turned to his stand partner again and said, "I can't hear myself. Am I playing?" As told later, it was very amusing. Of course, he was apologizing for his earlier comment.

She got caught in that disaster that was Rudolph Bing when he was head of the Metropolitan Opera. In spite of his apparent success here, Bing always deprecated the United States: nothing was ever as good here as in Europe—he was born in Austria and later spent time in England. It seemed that he did not wish to have any American singers at the Metropolitan Opera. The Wagner wing of the Met had been saved during World War II by the American soprano Helen Traubel, with her similarly big voice. When Herr Bing took over as manager he no longer used Traubel. Until the very end, he did not hire the spectacular coloratura Beverly Sills. It was only because of serious complaints that Rudolph Bing finally contracted Eileen Farrell for some dates at the opera house. He never had her sing the roles for which she was noted and so she eventually no longer went back.

She made many operatic recordings during her career, with conductors that included Leonard Bernstein, Thomas Shippers, and Max Rudolf. In addition she did some popular CDs, with a deep sinuous molding of the tunes. In 1971 she left the big solo opera career and moved to Bloomington, Indiana, where she was a Distinguished Professor of Music at Indiana University until 1980. She then taught at the University of Maine until 1985. She died in 2002 in Park Ridge, New Jersey.

A soprano who was often on the scene in Chicago was Kiri Te Kanawa. She was a beautiful lady with a sensible attitude, humorous and pleasant, originally from New Zealand. Solti used her in many operatic performances all over the world and in symphony productions and recordings. One year, Solti scheduled her for the Chicago Symphony concerts and for a recording of the *St. Matthew Passion* by Bach. Kiri Te Kanawa was singing the part of Pilate's wife.

In part 2 there is a touching aria for her, "For love, my savior now is dying," which has an extensive flute obbligato. I had performed this many times over the years with the CSO, at the Bach Festival in Carmel, California, at the Festival of Puerto Rico in San Juan, and in Carnegie Hall with Pablo Casals, as well as on recital and chamber music programs. I knew the aria very well, and I loved it. I was therefore surprised when, at the first rehearsal with Solti and Te Kanawa, the tempo was quite fast. Solti was always aware of everything on the stage. He noticed my reaction and called me into his dressing room at intermission. He said, "My dear, we must go with this faster tempo if you will. Kiri has never sung this work before and is quite anxious about it. I want her to be as comfortable as possible. So, would you mind doing her tempo?" I replied, "Of course I will." She also came to me backstage after one of the rehearsals and apologized for the tempo. I told her not to be concerned, that I would listen and accommodate to any tempo that she took. She continued, "I knew that I shouldn't have accepted this engagement. Solti talked me into it. He is *so* persuasive." She ended up sounding beautiful at the concerts and on the recording.

I think that she felt comfortable talking with me about the Bach because we'd met socially at a party the week before. I had said to her, "Miss Te Kanawa, my name is Donald Peck. I am the principal flute with the Chicago Symphony. I would love to speak with you." She said, "My name is Kiri Te Kanawa. I sing in opera houses." Of course, we both broke up laughing and had a wonderful conversation.

At the many performances that she sang with us over the years, I never saw behavior that wasn't professional and well mannered. This was the case even when she had to deal with the person who dubbed himself *thee* tenor, Luciano Pavarotti. Decca/London decided to record the Verdi opera *Otello* in Solti's final year as music director. The *Otello* concerts were in April of 1991, with two at Orchestra Hall in Chicago and two at Carnegie Hall in New York City. The recording was taken from those four performances. They had an exceptional cast, with Pavarotti, Te Kanawa, Leo Nucci, and Anthony Rolfe Johnson.

Pavarotti brought a lovely quality of tone to his arias, but his voice was a shade light for the role, so it was not in his usual repertoire. This may have been why he was not as familiar with his part as one would wish. Compounding the difficulty, Pavarotti does not read music. He learned everything by rote. C'mon, a self-proclaimed world-famous star! Why didn't he learn? Opera *is* music.

Solti was known to have a flamboyant temper, but we had not seen this side of him, as L'Orchestre de Paris and Covent Garden in London had. We saw it now, vis-à-vis Pavarotti. It was outrageous, the rehearsal time that was wasted going over and over sections so that Luciano could finally absorb them. What an insult to the other flawless singers, to Solti, and to the Chicago Symphony players, not to mention Verdi. Solti let fly several *very* loud castigations in his direction.

Other mannerisms Pavarotti affected during the proceedings included showing a complete lack of interest in the opera except when he was singing. He would slump in his chair, giving the impression that he was napping, as he may well have been. Even worse, however, in both rehearsal and concert he often peeled a banana and ate it, sometimes during another soloist's aria. Some audience members, catching me after a performance, asked what that was all about. I looked at the ceiling and shrugged.

To top off the whole prima-donna attitude, he refused to allow any of the other star singers to enter or leave the stage before him, even Kiri Te Kanawa. She just looked bemused and stood aside, to give his attitude first exit through the stage door. Many years earlier, in 1977, the CSO and Solti had been preparing to record the Verdi *Requiem*. The tenor was to have been Pavarotti, but he canceled, as he so often did all over the world. Veriano Luchetti replaced him.

Every few years I was involved in performances of the Mad scene from *Lucia di Lammermoor*, by Donizetti. This is an aria for coloratura soprano, with flute obbligato. I remember doing it with Lily Pons, Roberta Peters, Anna Moffo, Joan Sutherland, and others.

I came to know Anna Moffo when we were students at the Curtis Institute of Music in Philadelphia. She was very nice, quiet and almost shy. She usually wore a navy blue skirt, a white blouse, and a navy blue sweater. Under her arm were her music and schoolbooks, as her classwork had priority. I remember her excellence in the solfège class. She was attractive, yes, but not yet glamorous. Well! Ten years later, when she came to Ravinia as soloist with the Symphony, she was definitely super-glamorous, with a lithe body, stunning hair and clothes, and an eye-catching walk. By this time she had become a superstar with world engagements, but a base at the Metropolitan Opera.

We met to discuss the cadenza for *Lucia*, but spent most of the meeting remembering old times and catching up on new times. We had a wonderful visit. With all of her diva notoriety she was still the same sweet girl of the navy blue skirt.

She sounded simply marvelous at the concert, with none of the edginess some high sopranos display on the top of their range. She also had a mellow and sensual mid-to-lower octave. It was not a huge voice, but she guided her repertoire carefully to be sure to sing the operas that were proper for her voice. She died in March of 2006.

One of the best and most famous sopranos was Joan Sutherland, from Australia. She had a large voice, and thought at one time that she would go into the Wagner repertoire. However, Richard Bonygne, often her conductor and later her husband, urged her to utilize the flexibility that her voice possessed and do the bel canto repertoire. Although she was duly focused on her career and work, she gave the impression of being relaxed, and so was charming and witty. I went backstage at the Ravinia Festival to rehearse with her alone, to see how she did the *Lucia* aria. I felt insecure in one part of it and asked how she intended to sing that section. She observed me with that "wouldn't you like to know" look and said, "I really don't know, lovey. I'll have to wait until tonight to find out." Big laugh.

The outdoor evening concert arrived. The Mad scene turned out to be a mad scene for me. It was very windy that night, with strong gales coming up on the stage. I stood next to the conductor's podium up front so as to be next to Sutherland. She entered the stage wearing a multi-yarded, bright green, diaphanous gown, which was swishing with great theatricality all around her because of the wind. As we got into the music her gown was whipping all around me, my flute, and, worst of all, my music stand. I couldn't see a thing. Conductor Bonygne tried to push her flying shawl to one side, away from my stand, but to no avail. The wind was the master of the dress.

As it happens, I had played the cadenza often enough that the tiny occasional glimpse I could grab of the music got me through the experience. It was frightening, but also very funny. We laughed about it later backstage. Ms. Sutherland rewarded me with a bottle of champagne. I needed it!

And so we go from the sweet to the bitter: Maria Callas. Admittedly she had a huge following and reputation, but I feel these were not due to her singing. They were based on her emotive stage acting and her bizarre offstage behavior. To some people her voice was edgy and colorless, with a disturbingly wide vibrato. In the higher octaves, some said, the tone became thinner, more strident, and out of tune. She compensated for this by flagrant overacting on the stage. My reaction was that she should have become an actress only, without singing, as she did once in the play *Medea*.

During my first year in the orchestra, Callas came to Chicago for a concert. The Chicago Symphony was hired, as an extra job, to do her program. The rehearsal was scheduled for two hours, from 10 AM until noon. We were in our places at the prescribed time. But not so Maria Callas. We waited, and waited, and waited. No soprano.

At noon the rehearsal time had run out. The orchestra personnel stood up to leave. At just that moment the "diva" walked onto the stage. Her agent released a statement to the press that the orchestra had risen out of respect, to welcome her to the hall. What a manipulation of the truth! The manager of that concert asked the orchestra if we would please stay around for another two hours so that there could be a rehearsal. Most of us did, but it cost him a pretty penny, as we were paid at the overtime rate, which was not cheap.

During my coming-of-age days, I had two favorite pop singers: Chet Baker, who alternated a thoughtful, mellow trumpet sound with his melancholy singing, and Peggy Lee, who was a big star at that time. I had many LPs of both of these heroes of mine, but especially of Peggy Lee.

She was from a little town in North Dakota and had left home in her mid-teens because of family problems. Soon afterward, a popular bandleader, Benny Goodman, hired her. In a short time they had a big hit, "Why Don't You Do Right?" Her career was started! Later, on her own, she continued her rise to stardom. Songs like "Lover," "Mañana," and "Black Coffee" showed her diversity of style. In the '70s she came to Chicago to do some concerts. A friend of mine who played horn in the Lyric Opera Orchestra was hired for that job. He told me that if I planned to see the Peggy Lee show he would take me backstage at intermission to meet her. What a thrill!

A few weeks before the show, returning to Chicago from an out-of-town concert, I was in a rather serious car accident. My throat bashed into the steering wheel. For two weeks I couldn't speak. At the time of Lee's show I could finally make sounds again, but they were more like a frog croaking than like speech. So hornist Paul took me backstage at intermission, and there was Peggy! He introduced me as from the CSO. She graciously greeted me and held out her hand for me to shake. I was in heaven. Then I spoke, saying how very happy I was to meet her. She looked horrified when she heard my croak. She was always nervous about getting colds that would hamper her singing. She gasped, turned around, and walked away quickly. I don't blame her a bit, of course, but I was devastated! After all those years, sob sob sob. Fate can be cruel. My voice was fine the next week. The Wrong Place; The Wrong Time, wouldn't you say?

It is impossible to list all of the great vocal performances that I am proud to have been a part of with the Chicago Symphony. A few that come to mind are Kiri Te Kanawa in Brahms's *Requiem*, Mahler's Fourth Symphony, and Strauss's *Four Last Songs* with Solti; René Kollo in excerpts from *Tristan* with Solti; Thomas Hampson in Brahms's *Requiem* with Barenboim, and in *Don Giovanni* with Levine; Siegfried Jerusalem and Waltraud Meier doing and recording *Das Lied von der Erde* by Mahler, with

Barenboim; Lisa Della Casa, in Mahler's Fourth Symphony with Reiner; Leontyne Price, in the Verdi *Requiem* with Solti, and arias with Reiner; and Monserrat Caballé, in Strauss's *Four Last Songs* with Irwin Hoffman. I have only mentioned a small group out of the large number. But the idea is there that I was indeed happy to have been around during this "right" time.

9

Knowing Some Soloists

$\mathcal{T}$he list of famous performers who appeared with the Chicago Symphony Orchestra is awesome. It was rewarding to work with them. Each had a different style of behavior. Some were courteous but withdrawn; others wanted to mingle with the orchestra members as part of the team. I became socially acquainted with a few of these over the years.

Early on was pianist John Browning. He was a big star from the '60s to the '90s and appeared with us almost every season, either downtown or at Ravinia. Samuel Barber's Piano Concerto had been written for him, so he did that with us on several occasions. Mozart concerti were also big on his list, as were the Rachmaninoff Rhapsody on a Theme of Paganini, the Beethoven Concerto no. 5, and Concerto no. 3 by Prokofiev.

He was one of many pianists who had been influenced by Vladimir Horowitz, having a fantastic technique and a tone of great clarity and brightness with no trace of muddiness even when using the pedal. I went to Orchestra Hall one afternoon to pick up something from my locker. Browning was on the stage with three twelve-foot grand pianos. He asked me to listen out front and give him my opinion as to which one had the cleanest sound, while still projecting a beautiful tone. He played all three for me and I told him I thought that piano number two met his goal, with a clear and beautiful timbre. "Good," he said, "that is exactly what I feel, but I am so inexperienced that I need some professional corroboration." He always had to have his little joke, as I learned after I got to know him. That was his modus operandi, slightly high-strung or almost edgy, and then he would smooth everything out with a cute witticism. We adjourned to a pleasant bar on the lower level of the Palmer House Hotel, just around the corner from Orchestra Hall, had two vodka martinis each, and got to know each other. We had many happy social occasions over the years in Chicago and New York, where he lived. He died in 2003.

A major star was flutist James Galway. He was from Northern Ireland but studied in London with the wonderful Geoffrey Gilbert. He played at different times with the London Symphony and the Royal Philharmonic before going to Berlin for six years as principal flutist with the Philharmonic. He then decided to try the field of solo flute and was a quick success in a big way. We became acquainted and friendly because of his first solo date with the Chicago Symphony in the John Corigliano Flute Concerto.

At that time, Corigliano was the composer-in-residence of the Chicago Symphony Orchestra. We were playing many works by him, conducted by both Sir Georg Solti and Daniel Barenboim. His Symphony no. 1 was written on commission for the CSO. We gave the first performance and recorded it on the Erato label with Barenboim conducting.

So the management called me in and asked if I would be interested in playing the Corigliano Flute Concerto. I looked at the score and found much entrancing music, but I had also seen a TV concert in which Galway had performed it with an orchestra. The concerto has the subtitle "Pied Piper." It uses that tale as a format. The flutist enters the hall from the back of the audience dressed in weird pants and a cape and treks down the aisle to the stage, all the time followed by seventy-nine or so little children. Maybe the children are the rats and the flutist is the Pied Piper: or maybe this is when the Pied Piper is leading the children away from Hamelin, never to return.

In any case, this was not for me. I went to Corigliano and told him how beautiful his music was in the concerto and that it didn't need the "show business" routine to carry it. Did he feel that it could be performed without the little children and a cape? He looked genuinely thoughtful and said that he would consider it and get back to me. Of course, he said no. He wanted the machinations. I got back to management and explained my reticence about performing the work. I recommended that they ask James Galway to do the piece. He knew the concerto. It had been written for him. And he looked good in a lavender cape. So that is the reason Jimmy came to the Chicago Symphony the first time. Actually, he did look good in the cape as he led the kiddies down the aisle to the stage.

He and I hit it off from the start. He is very friendly and down-to-earth. We had many lunches on his subsequent recital trips to Chicago. On occasion he would drop by my condominium. He always wanted to try flutes, so I dragged mine out for him. He was playing gold at this time. I was playing platinum, and had for years. My instrument fascinated him. I left him in the living room and he played on and on. Very soon after, his flute company made a platinum flute for him. It gave him a deeper, darker, fuller tone. He then recorded the Bach Sonatas on his platinum flute and continued to use it, in conjunction with the gold.

An episode occurred that is sad and amusing, and shows his generosity. On one of his trips we were at my home. He had a large case full of flutes, all gold. He took one out, told me to play it, and said how well it suited me. He wanted to leave it for me to experiment with. It was a good flute and I did enjoy it. On a TV tape that we made with Solti, performing Beethoven's Symphony no. 5, I played the platinum flute on the "big" first and final movements, and the gold flute on the melodic, quieter second and third movements. After the session Solti called me in to speak. "My dear," he said, "you sound lovely on the gold flute, and you were right to use it on the slow movement. But you really sound *vunderful* on the platinum in the other movements. Dot is for you!" I too liked platinum.

Jimmy had given me his gold flute in January. We spoke on the phone a few times later and he said to keep it longer; he was in no hurry. But come July, I really felt that I had to get it back to him! He was at the Tanglewood Festival. I phoned him and said that I wanted to return his flute. He said to wait, that I was coming to Lucerne, his home, in September on tour with the orchestra and I could bring it with me then. But I said no, I was nervous about keeping it so long. He said okay—send it to him at Tanglewood. And I did. He then left Tanglewood and returned to Lucerne.

The next day he phoned me from there. He screamed at me on the phone—in a joking manner, I hasten to add. He explained, "When I got off the plane in Lucerne, I put my case of twelve flutes on a cart and went to the regular baggage area. When I returned, the cart and all the flutes were gone—stolen! I have no flute. If you had kept my flute a week longer, I would at least now have one flute!"

I guess that he was right. Nevertheless, I feel sure that his attentive flute maker got him an instrument pronto. We kept track of this event for some time but never heard what had happened to the flutes or who had taken them. At least it didn't interfere with our genial lunches or after-concert get-togethers. He is now Sir James Galway.

A solo flutist that I came to think of as an acquaintance was Jean-Pierre Rampal. He was the first new flute soloist to emerge after World War II and had a successful career. He was in Chicago many times, often doing recitals in adjacent towns while staying in Chicago hotels. He was never a soloist with the symphony but often attended orchestra rehearsals or concerts and would come backstage to say hello. Like Galway, he was interested in the platinum flute and seemed to enjoy trying mine. He never took to it quite as strongly as Jimmy, however, as his French musical background and ear didn't allow for the depth and emotion of that metal.

I finally won him over with another metal, a French automobile. I drove to a Chicago suburb, Evanston, to hear him play a flute recital. Afterward I went backstage to greet him. He was his usual friendly self and asked me if I would give him a ride back to Chicago and to his hotel, the Drake, near my condominium. After speaking with his recital fans we walked out into a sunny afternoon, down the street to my car. Arriving at it, Rampal stopped dead in his tracks, turned to me with a quivering mouth, and was speechless!

For a number of years I had been driving this French car, a 1979 Citroën, brilliant blue. I loved it more than any car I have ever owned. It had no springs, but rather air-oil suspension. After the engine was turned on, the car would be pumped up onto its oil base. It had a most fabulous ride and control. When the engine was turned off, the car would sink down into itself again. Citroëns never became popular in the United States. They were too different-looking for Americans to accept. To be honest, they rather looked like an inverted bathtub. We had been seduced by General Motors' advertising into preferring the gross appearance of their cars at that time. In the mid-'80s, Peugot, another French automobile maker, bought Citroën and proceeded to make them look like every other car on the road. I thought it was very sad.

In any case, Rampal loved my Citroën. I had the feeling that his respect for me had leaped up a few hundred percent. We had a warm conversation over the twenty miles back to his hotel. But don't you think it is odd that he didn't ask me in for a glass of French wine?

A glorious array of violinists appeared as soloists during my career with the Chicago Symphony Orchestra: Jascha Heifetz, Nathan Milstein, Zino Francescatti, Isaac Stern, Itzhak Perlman, Pinchas Zukerman.

Zukerman in his middle years took up conducting. He was music director of the St. Paul Chamber Orchestra before moving on to the Ottawa Chamber Orchestra. He was a magnificent violinist, lyrical and limpid, never too forceful or edgy. By 1977 I was getting a bit tired of the Beethoven Violin Concerto, which we played very often. But when Zukerman came that year and performed it with Barenboim conducting, I became entranced with the work again. He gave a lyrical, commanding performance: honest, sweet music making. The recording we made at that time is certainly the one that I like most to hear.

As a guest conductor of the Chicago Symphony over many years, he had strong musical purposes he wished to express. He always related to us in a firm but gentlemanly way. So as to make the concert seem like a performance of chamber music, he never used a podium. He stood on the floor at orchestra level and waved the baton only when needed. I enjoyed working with him. My final performance with the Symphony was with him conducting Dvořák's Symphony no. 8.

I often saw Zukerman after a concert in the restaurant-lounge establishment in the Orchestra Hall building, called Rhapsody. We visited each other's tables and chatted about the just-finished concert, or next season, or the weather. Four years after I left the orchestra I went to a concert that he conducted. Afterward, as I was sitting in Rhapsody with some friends, he walked in. He saw me at the table and came over. He called me by name and spoke of some of the repertoire that we had performed together in the past. Again that weird feeling about the sharp brains of many conductors. How did he remember all of that?

Another magnificent violinist who soloed with us almost every season was Isaac Stern. We appreciated his approach to each concerto and how he listened to, and meshed with, the orchestra. He was not a ham. He was an outstanding musician.

My first professional and personal moment with him came after a rehearsal of the Tchaikovsky Violin Concerto during one of my early years in the orchestra. At intermission he came to me and said that my flute solo at the beginning of the second movement was certainly one of the most touching interpretations that he had ever heard. He added that it gave him some ideas as to how he should phrase it when the melody appeared in the violin part. You can imagine my surprise and joy at these remarks, as I was yet a young lad finding my way. That was very generous of him. We always spoke together during his later engagements, sometimes adjourning to a coffee-wine-food bistro directly next door to the hall.

One of our big topics was the Prokofiev Sonata no. 2 for violin and piano. This work was written in 1943 as a sonata for flute and piano, op. 94. Prokofiev made the version for violin and piano for violinist David Oistrakh in 1944 as op. 94b. A few alterations were made to suit the violin, but it is essentially the same work. I listened to recordings by violinists and tried to duplicate their essence on the flute when I performed it. Isaac Stern's recording was my favorite.

One year he performed as soloist with the Symphony in the Thursday, Friday, and Saturday concerts. On Sunday afternoon he then gave a violin recital, including the Prokofiev Sonata. Naturally I went to this concert. Reaching the backstage area after the program, I saw him throw his hands up over his head in mock horror at my presence. "What are *you* doing here?" he belted out. I replied that I came to hear his recital, especially the Prokofiev. "That's what I was afraid of" were his next words. He explained that he had only put the Prokofiev on the program because someone had requested it. He hadn't played it in months and would never have programmed it if he had known that I was coming to the recital. I told him that it had been absolutely beautiful, that he had given me a few ideas for future phrasing of my own. I thought that was a genial way of returning the favor of his remark to me on the Tchaikovsky Concerto's second movement a few years earlier.

We must honor Isaac Stern for his achievements as the driving force behind the preservation of Carnegie Hall in the '70s, when some developers were going to raze it and build an apartment building on the site. How strange this seems, when we consider all of the small, tacky buildings in the area that could have been torn down and never missed. He gathered a group of fellow musicians and music lovers to fight the proposal. Extra concerts with much press coverage gave the situation notoriety and raised enough money to deal with the matter. The greatest concert hall in the world was saved!

The musician responsible for the style and sound of American flute playing is William Kincaid. He joined the Philadelphia Orchestra in 1921 at the age of twenty-six. In 1928 he joined the staff of the Curtis Institute of Music, where he coached a crop of flutists over the years, and they attained most of the positions in orchestras in the United States. Principal players included Joseph Mariano in Rochester; Julius Baker in New York; Maurice Sharp, Cleveland; Emil Opava, Minneapolis; Albert Tipton, Detroit; Jacob Berg, St. Louis; Byron Hester, Houston; Doriot Dwyer, Boston; Donald Peck, Chicago; and many more. In turn, these players turned out their students with the Kincaid aura still intact, though altered a bit by their own personalities. Especially notable on the list of teachers of influence were Joseph Mariano at the Eastman School, and Julius Baker at the Julliard School and later the Curtis Institute.

The Kincaid vision of flute playing leaned toward a deeper, more important tone than had been the style before him. He wanted to play in a musical way, not just make birdcalls or chirpy ego phrases. It was a violinistic approach to music, meant to rescue the woodwinds from sounding uninvolved or unimportant. His students picked up on this, as is apparent in the huge, sensual, round tone of Mariano, and the lovely, centered, but full sound of Baker.

Kincaid was a bit removed from his students when they were at the Curtis Institute, but after they graduated he became quite friendly. When I was in Washington, D.C., for three years I liked to go up to Philadelphia for a weekend. I often met Kincaid after a concert. We always went around the corner of Fifteenth and Spruce, near the Academy of Music, to have a few drinks at an Irish pub. I would have a beer; Kincaid always had Haig and Haig scotch. There were some fascinating conversations about the musical world. I felt honored to be there. He left the orchestra in 1960 and died in 1967. From him came a legacy that influenced the whole world of music.

10

Making Recordings

$\mathcal{A}$ boon to the recording industry, orchestras, and listeners was the introduction of the long-playing record, the LP, by Columbia Records in 1948. Previously one had to deal with the 78 RPM (revolutions per minute) disc. This was a twelve-inch disc of shellac, scratchy and easily breakable, with only four minutes of playing time per side. A thirty-minute work took four discs. One had to turn a disc over or listen to the needle crash down on a record changer every few minutes.

The LP, at 33⅓ RPM, was made of unbreakable vinyl. With the smaller grooves and slower speed there was very little, if any, needle scratch. The best attribute, though, was the thirty-minute duration of each side. The sound was fuller and deeper, and heralded the High Fidelity era.

RCA sought to compete with Columbia and came out with its own product, a 45 RPM disc. This was better than the 78s, but not as good as the 33s. After a few years they dropped it and joined the LP bandwagon, as did record companies throughout the world. The entire repertoire that had previously been on 78s was re-recorded on 33s, as were a host of new works. Orchestras, conductors, and soloists were much in demand. Record companies and record shops were doing big business.

New recording companies were formed to cash in on the bonanza. Capitol Records, which had formerly been in the pop-tune field, signed the St. Louis Symphony under Vladimir Golschmann, and the Los Angeles Philharmonic with Alfred Wallenstein and an occasional Erich Leinsdorf. A new American company was formed, Mercury Records, which contracted the Detroit Symphony, conducted by Paul Paray, the Minneapolis Symphony with Antal Dorati, and the Chicago Symphony under then music director Rafael Kubelik. The other major U.S. orchestras were divided up between Columbia and RCA.

The recordings by Mercury-Chicago were outstanding and are still available in the shops, now transferred to CDs. Monaural recording was the standard then, so these discs were taped with but one microphone, placed in an optimum position over the orchestra. In this way the performance of the players was captured, instead of one devised by the producer-engineer, as later occurred with the multi-microphone system of stereophonic sound. A special recording of Kubelik and the Chicago Symphony from this period is *Pictures at an Exhibition*, by Mussorgsky.

Kubelik did not stay long in Chicago. Fritz Reiner took over as music director in 1953, at which time the orchestra switched to RCA for recording. I was not in Chicago for his first four years, but joined the CSO in 1957. I was surprised at the amount of recording that the orchestra was doing. It even grew in the ensuing forty-two years of my tenure. Over that expanse of time we recorded three hundred issues of LPs and CDs. An issue is one disc, but it usually included more than one musical selection. Thus, we recorded through that period 490 pieces of music. We worked with twenty-two conductors and twelve recording companies. Being in the right place at the right time doesn't hurt at all.

Many of the Fritz Reiner recordings from that era have become famous. They were transferred to CDs and repeatedly re-issued. One of these was a 1959 recording of Rimsky-Korsakov's *Scheherazade* suite. This was not Reiner's usual métier, so he studied the music carefully and decided to present it as a fine work of art instead of the usual show-off piece. He was especially effective in the third movement, taking it slower than usual, with a touching sensitivity. RCA featured the first-chair players, naming them on the LP cover and later on the CD's.

We recorded a wide spectrum of composers: Respighi tone poems; Debussy's *La mer*; Berlioz's *Nuits d'été* with Leontyne Price; a Spanish album, again with Price, doing *El amor brujo*, by de Falla; Richard and Johann Strauss; many concerti with Van Cliburn as pianist (Reiner really liked him, treating him in a fatherly fashion); Prokofiev; Wagner; Tchaikovsky; Beethoven; Mahler's *Das Lied von der Erde* and his Fourth Symphony—an amazing array of different styles.

In 1962 we had a session of Richard Strauss with the tone poems *Also sprach Zarathustra* and *Don Juan*. We played through *Don Juan* in one take.

It was magnificent! At the finish, Reiner sat on the podium looking completely fulfilled.

Then the RCA producer, Richard Mohr, who was the best ever, spoke to the maestro via the loudspeakers: "Dr. Reiner, would you mind doing a small section over again for us?" Reiner scowled and growled, "No, it was wonderful. No more!" There was a long silence. Dick Mohr then said that it was indeed wonderful, but just a few measures, please, as a car had gone by on the street and its noise had intruded into the hall.

Reiner was very unhappy. He said that he would listen to the playback and then make a decision. The engineers started the playback from the beginning, and it *was* very special. But in the middle of the work, we heard a cracked note from one of the French horn players. That really had been what Mohr was talking about, but he hadn't said it so as not to embarrass a horn player or influence Reiner. Fritz liked to run things himself. He told Richard to stop the tape and replay it. Again we heard the horn blooper. Reiner looked at Dick Mohr with his little, uncanny eyes, and said, "Is that the automobile horn?" Mohr sheepishly admitted that it was, so Reiner agreed to do eight measures over. That is the only splice in the whole performance, which is an ecstatic one.

A few other conductors recorded with the orchestra during the Reiner years. A famous glory of the violin, Jascha Heifetz, had a disagreement with Fritz Reiner a few years after Reiner came to Chicago, so when Heifetz wanted to record the Sibelius Violin Concerto with the Chicago Symphony Orchestra, the assistant conductor, Walter Hendl, was asked to do the taping. Heifetz and Hendl had worked together previously when Hendl was the music director of the Dallas Symphony, recording the Rózsa Violin Concerto.

Heifetz came to Orchestra Hall on January 10, 1959, for six hours of recording, 10 AM to 1 PM, and 7 to 10 PM. He played the first movement of the Sibelius completely through with no stops. It was wonderful! Then he started in. "I must do this again, I must do that again." This took us into the evening session just finishing up the first movement. We then got into the second movement with the same care. When the six-hour day ended, we had only done two movements. We were told to return on Monday morning at 10 AM for a four-hour session. At least we had Sunday free.

After working for three hours on the third movement Monday morning, we sighed with relief. We thought that we were finished. After all, we did have a 3 PM orchestra rehearsal. We were naïve. Heifetz announced that he wished to play the complete concerto through, like a performance, utilizing the fourth hour. So we did. Heifetz had started out on Saturday AM playing beautifully. Into the tenth hour of recording Sibelius, on Monday, he played magnificently! That final run-through was as if from a god. The RCA producer told me some months later that the issue of the Sibelius was almost completely that final take, with only a few minor inserts.

Hendl did other recordings with us, among them the Lalo *Symphonie espagnole* with Henry Szerying, and a Van Cliburn album of the MacDowell no. 2 and Prokofiev no. 3 piano concerti. He was a very pleasant man, who finished his career as the head of the Eastman School of Music. This was the time when we did the famous Franck Symphony LP with Pierre Monteux, discussed in chapter 5, "Guest Conductors." But RCA concentrated mainly on Fritz Reiner. Between 1957 and 1964 the company made twenty-seven issues of Reiner/CSO recordings. Most of them are still on the market.

Fritz Reiner left the orchestra in the fall of 1962, and Jean Martinon came as music director in the fall of 1964. RCA was a bit concerned, as Martinon was not well known in America. He agreed that other conductors could do some of the recordings to fulfill the contract. Nevertheless, in November of Martinon's first season we recorded with him Ravel's *Daphnis and Chloe* suite no. 2, the orchestra's first of three recordings we did of this work over the years, and Roussel's suite no. 2 from *Bacchus et Ariane*. It is a fine performance, done in the expansive sound that Orchestra Hall provided at that time. It has now been issued as a CD.

In ensuing months Morton Gould came to conduct. He recorded his *Spirituals for Orchestra* and the Copland *Dance* symphony. This was the first of many recordings by him and the orchestra over the next few years. RCA brought in Seiji Ozawa, music director at the Ravinia Festival, to record with us in the summer months beginning in 1965. Martinon resumed his recording in the spring of 1966 with the Concerto for seven winds, by Frank Martin. We saw Morton Gould in June, to tape Nielsen's Symphony no. 2.

And then the problem began. For many years, it was thought that Orchestra Hall should be renovated to generally stabilize the structure, which had been built in the early 1900s. The hall sounded wonderful as a recording venue, as demonstrated on all of the Kubelik and Reiner issues. For concerts, although it was never bad, it became somewhat dry, since the audience absorbed too much of the sound. So the renovation was done in the summer of 1966.

The acousticians decided that the space was too small and devised a plan whereby the ceiling would be removed and replaced with a screen. The hall would still have the same look. We were told that the sound would go up into the rafters, reverberate, and come back down more glorious than ever. The sound indeed went up into the rafters. Unfortunately, it stayed there. Now we *really* had a dry hall.

The orchestra came back in October of '66 for the new season. Jean Martinon arrived to rehearse the opening program, which started with the Beethoven overture *The Consecration of the House*, in honor of the "new" hall. He gave the downbeat. We played the loud chord. It sounded: THUMP! And that was it. There was no quality to the tone, no reverberation, just one dead lump of sound. The Nielsen Symphony no. 4 was also on this program. RCA entered the scene on October 10 to record it. They were appalled at the acoustics in a place that had been famous for its recording quality. They manipulated the equipment, adding some echo and a bit more treble. But, as well as the piece had been played, it was never an outstanding recording. RCA gave the hall one more trial in December, realized that it was no longer the place to use, and searched for another recording venue. Don't you love those acousticians?

A few blocks south of Orchestra Hall is the Auditorium Theatre. It was built by Louis Sullivan, a famous Chicago architect, in the early 1900s. RCA decided to try this hall for our next recording with Morton Gould in February of 1966, an album of the music of Charles Ives. The stage was too confining a space, so it too did not work well for recording. So back to Orchestra Hall on March 8 for the Schumann Piano Concerto, with pianist Artur Rubinstein and conductor Carlo Maria Giulini. RCA had adapted a bit to the new acoustics, so the quality of this recording was better than that of the two previous ones, but it was still not right. The search continued.

In April and May we were in a third space, Medinah Temple. This hall had almost too much reverberation, so they had to record us fairly close, otherwise the sound would have been muddy. The tone quality lacked depth, but it was certainly the best space we had been in recently. Jean Martinon recorded Bartók's *Miraculous Mandarin* and Mendelssohn's *Midsummer Night's Dream* at this time. Medinah Temple was to be our main recording venue for several years.

The '67–'68 season was a busy recording year. We had sessions with Ozawa, George Pretre, several with Martinon, and a most exciting experience, making two LPs with Leopold Stokowski, one featuring the Khatchaturian Symphony no. 3 and another the Shostakovich Symphony no. 6. He never asked us to do anything specific with the quality of tone; he merely evoked his special sound, so gorgeous in the strings and sweet in the winds. Amazing!

Also on the 1968 schedule was the taping of two symphonies with Morton Gould, the Rimsky-Korsakov Symphony no. 2 (*Antar*) and Miaskovsky's Symphony no. 21. These works are rarely played at concerts—why? They are exciting, beautifully orchestrated, and filled with lovely melodies. This was the first and only time I ever performed them.

In spite of all of the problems at Orchestra Hall, RCA had us back there in July and August of 1968. We recorded with Ozawa Schubert's Symphony no. 8, Tchaikovsky's Symphony no. 5, Beethoven's Symphony no. 5, and Stravinsky's *The Rite of Spring*. In the summer of 1969, Ozawa returned, this time with Angel/EMI Records. They didn't want to use Medinah Temple and took us to a far Western suburb called Wheaton, to Edman Chapel. We spent one whole day there recording Kodály's *Dances of Galánta* and Borodin's *Polovtsian Dances*. Nothing could be used from that session because of the acoustics. We weren't too unhappy, as we had been paid for a full day of recording. A few days later, on June 30 and July 1, Angel did go into Medinah Temple to re-do the Borodin and Kodály and to add Rimsky-Korsakov's *Scheherazade* and Bartók's Concerto for orchestra. This was a lot of recording in only two days, but we did it.

We were there again in October for Angel, with Giulini scheduled for three days to record Berlioz's *Romeo and Juliet*, and the Stravinsky *Firebird* and *Petrouchka* suites. Those sessions went so well, and so quickly, that there was a day left over. We had recently performed the Brahms Symphony no. 4 with Giulini, so Angel took advantage of that and threw it in on the extra time. Performing this music without having to rehearse it made it very fresh to us. The recording is absolutely beautiful, capturing Giulini's deep maroon orchestra tone and tragic inner feeling.

Try as they may, conductors cannot do every piece of music in an exalted fashion. The very things that made Giulini's Brahms so gripping are the things that were not proper for his Stravinsky. *Petrouchka* especially needs a bright and clear sound with incisive attacks; we often called it the "bite" of Stravinsky. We recorded the *Firebird* in later years with Pierre Boulez and it is wonderful. Likewise, we made two other CDs of the *Petrouchka* ballet, with Levine and Solti. They are more persuasive than that of Giulini. These comments are not intended to demean Giulini, of whom, as you will have gathered, we were very fond. It is only to state some facts about the irony of making music; proper style and proper approach must have precedence over the performer's innate feelings.

Georg Solti, not yet Sir Georg, became the music director in the fall of 1969. He made a few recordings for RCA during his life, but his primary company was from England: Decca/London. His first recording session was on March 26, 27, and 31, 1970. We did Mahler's Symphony no. 5. I found it fascinating that our premier effort with him was to become our theme song, our banner over the years. On April 1, 5, 6, 7, and 8 we continued with Mahler: the Symphony no. 6, *Des Knaben Wunderhorn*, and *Songs of a Wayfarer* with Yvonne Minton, mezzo-soprano, all done at Medinah Temple.

The year 1970 saw the beginning of Solti in Chicago and the end of Ozawa, who left his Ravinia position to become music director of the San Francisco Symphony. Our final session with him was on June 29, for Angel. We recorded, in one three-hour period, the Janáček *Sinfonietta* and the Lutoslawski Concerto for orchestra.

An amusing incident occurred at a recording session in November of 1970. As a guest conductor, Daniel Barenboim directed Dvořák's cello concerto, with his wife, Jacqueline du Pré, as soloist. A good friend of "Danny's" was Pinchas Zukerman, who was in Chicago at the time. He came to listen to the recording session. This was on Angel Records at Medinah Temple.

Six hours had been scheduled. "Pinky" stayed around for all of it. At one of the playback-listening periods late in the day, Zukerman lifted his head and said to Barenboim, "Oh, I have finally figured out what you and Jackie are doing." Barenboim looked startled and asked, "What do you mean?" Pinky answered, "You are making a *two*-record set!" We all broke up laughing, including Danny and Jackie. Zukerman was teasing them about the tempos, which were very, very slow.

We hit a big Mahler stride in 1971, starting with Giulini, on Angel, doing the Symphony no. 1 along with Beethoven's Symphony no. 7, and continuing with Solti on Decca/London recording Mahler's Symphonies no. 7 and no. 8. The companies continually attempted to find other halls in which to record, so the Mahler Seventh was done at the University of Illinois's Krannert Center in Champaign-Urbana, 150 miles south of Chicago. We did two Beethoven piano concerti, no. 3 and no. 5, the same week, with Vladimir Ashkenazy. I have told the story of recording the Mahler Symphony no. 8 with chorus and soloists in Vienna in chapter 3, "Touring the World."

Decca/London temporarily had a preference for Krannert Center. It was a modern concert hall, sounding quite spacious out in the audience section. On the stage it was very mellow, with too much reverberation. To those of us placed at the middle and back of the stage, the sound was not clear. The string players often like this type of hall, as it makes them sound more glamorous and full-bodied, as in the Concertgebouw in Amsterdam and Symphony Hall in Boston. The wind players usually feel a lack of definition in their tone, making it difficult to hear the proper pitches and to find the correct balance.

Nevertheless, there we were for several days in May of 1972 with a large agenda; Mahler's *Das Lied von der Erde*, Beethoven's Symphony no. 9, shuttling our large CSO Chorus all the way south from Chicago, doing the remainder of the piano concerti with Ashkenazy—1, 2 and 4, Berlioz's *Symphonie fantastique*, Strauss's *Don Juan*, and four overtures. Whew! I'm tired just reading about it.

That wasn't all for 1972. On November 1 we recorded the first of what was to become a cycle of the Bruckner symphonies with guest conductor Daniel Barenboim. On that day we were back at Medinah Temple doing the Fourth Symphony, with a new label for us, Deutsche Grammophon. We developed a friendly and respectful relationship with DG, taping many albums for them with Barenboim, Giulini, Abbado, and Levine. The days of monogamous marriages between orchestras and record companies had passed. We were among the most faithless, but our bank accounts loved it.

It got to be tiresome running here and there looking for a new hall in which to record, especially since we always ended up back at Medinah Temple. That's where we were in 1973 and 1974. Having done Beethoven's Symphony no. 9 the previous year, we now completed the cycle with Georg Solti. He also did Stravinsky's *Rite of Spring* and the Elgar *Enigma Variations*. In '74 James Levine made his recording debut with us on RCA, doing Mahler's Symphony no. 4.

The next two years, '75 and '76, were extremely busy recording times. We had Solti on Decca, Levine on RCA doing the four Brahms symphonies, Barenboim on DG, and Giulini on Angel-EMI. In 1976, we made our first recording with Claudio Abbado conducting, on DG. He did the Mahler Symphony no. 2. Also in that year, we had a very exciting event, our first recording of a complete opera: Wagner's *The Flying Dutchman*, with Solti conducting, and a cast including Norman Bailey, Janis Martin, and Rene Kollo. More opera issues from us were to follow.

It was becoming apparent that the first recording with Solti, Mahler's Symphony no. 5, had made us the "Mahler orchestra." Not only was Solti finishing up his cycle of eight Mahler symphonies, but Abbado, Levine, Giulini, and eventually Barenboim all jumped on our bandwagon to take advantage of our renown. This was a great experience for us, as it made it very clear that the same work should not be played exactly the same way each time. Each director had a different approach to Mahler, and so the musicians changed their performance. It was not just a repetition of the notes. Nineteen seventy-seven was another huge year of recording with all of the above conductors, plus the addition of another one: André Previn, who did the Shostakovich Symphonies nos. 4 and 5 on the Angel label. Two large choral works were recorded by Solti: the Beethoven *Missa solemnis*, on Decca, and the Verdi *Requiem*, on RCA. Chapter 3 tells the story of the Verdi *Requiem* preceding a tour to Japan.

The Chicago Symphony did not usually record works of small orchestration. The cost was high, since every player was paid a fee even if he did not make the record. So it was gratifying for us to record for RCA the Bach Brandenburg Concerti no. 2 and no. 5, especially since these had solo parts for flute, oboe, violin, and trumpet. James Levine played at the keyboard and conducted from there. We had hopes of doing the other three concerti, but it was not to be.

Another recording done with James Levine in 1977 was the complete *Petrouchka* ballet. Jimmy was very good on this music, as his incisive beat made it all extremely clear, which is what Stravinsky himself told us was needed for presenting his music. The ballet also had a story, so Levine could follow that when interpreting the music.

The story has a Showman of the circus playing a wooden flute one night to relax with his puppet, Petrouchka, after a day's work. The spontaneous tune that the Showman evokes from his instrument enchants the puppet. He comes to life. That music is a flute cadenza in Stravinsky's score. It can be very touching. Jimmy did three takes of it during the taping and asked me which take I would like him to use on the finished recording. I didn't know which one to choose. He laughed and said that it was different each time I played it, not only for the recording but all during my life, as it should be. I returned the laugh and said, "Yes." He suggested that I let him choose. A year later, when he had returned, he came over to me to ask if I liked the take that he had used on the CD. How did he remember that for the whole year?

Once we had done the *Requiems* of Verdi and Beethoven, the powers must have decided that we shouldn't slight Brahms. So in 1978 Solti recorded the *German Requiem*, with Kiri Te Kanawa, soprano. We also started the cycle of Brahms symphonies with Solti, no. 3 and no. 4, with no. 1 and no. 2 in 1979. That year had another exciting event, the recording with Solti of our second opera, Beethoven's *Fidelio*. It had a wonderful cast, including Hildegarde Behrens, Peter Hofmann, and Theo Adam.

Columbia Records returned in the fall with Erich Leinsdorf and pianist Lazar Berman for the Brahms Piano Concerto no. 1, which I discussed in chapter 5, "Guest Conductors." Solti began his Bruckner cycle with no. 6, while Barenboim was continuing his, and Abbado was doing his Mahler. As for us, we were becoming even more neurotic. It was not to end.

In 1980 and 1981 we felt like we were living in Vienna, as four conductors over the two years did numerous symphonies by the Austrians Mahler and Bruckner: Solti, Barenboim, Levine, and Abbado. We had a little relief in 1981, as the big item for Sir Georg that year was his taping of the Berlioz opera *La damnation de Faust*, featuring Kenneth Riegel and Frederica von Stade.

At some recording sessions the scheduled music might be completed before the allotted time was used up. The orchestra library would then be requested to bring to the stage some music that was not programmed for the recording. This would be standard repertoire, so that the lack of rehearsal would be no problem. We recorded it "cold turkey." In 1981 it was an all-Russian CD with Barenboim: Tchaikovsky's *Romeo and Juliet*, *Marche slave*, *1812 Overture*, and *Francesca da Rimini*, plus Rimsky-Korsakov's *Capriccio espagnol*. The orchestra made several "off the cuff" recordings over the years, four with Barenboim alone. I have already mentioned the Brahms Fourth Symphony, with Carlo Maria Giulini. Whenever this spontaneous recording situation occurred, the orchestra joked that the conductor, whoever it might be, didn't have any rehearsal time to ruin the performance!

In an attempt to improve the acoustics in Orchestra Hall, a series of new renovations were made in the mid-seventies, during the summer months. They put some panels in the rafters behind the false ceiling screens in an attempt to direct some of the sound back into the hall. It was somewhat successful, and so the recording-location "fun and games" began again. Decca and RCA continued on at Medinah Temple for a few years, while DG and Angel-EMI returned to Orchestra Hall. Finally in 1981 Decca made the move back to the Hall, with RCA joining the crowd in 1983. The acoustics had been improved a good deal, with more reverberation and feedback so it was more comfortable for us to record there.

More Solti/Mahler in 1982, but truly outstanding was his recording of suites 1 and 2 from Prokofiev's *Romeo and Juliet*. He really "got into" it, and so did the orchestra. It was one of those good days.

We were confused in 1983 by James Levine's profusion of record labels. He came in with his usual RCA, doing the Brahms *Requiem* and a piano concerto. Next he was with DG and doing Schubert's Ninth Symphony, followed by Phillips, a new company for us, and the five piano concerti of Beethoven with pianist Alfred Brendel. More of the same from Claudio

Abbado, with his usual DG dates, and then a CBS (formerly Columbia) session of Rachmaninoff's Piano Concerto no. 2 with Cecile Licad. We jokingly felt sorry for Solti, recording only on Decca, with a rare RCA venture. Interesting, though, was the thought that we now had two complete sets of the five Beethoven piano concerti on the market, plus several single discs with various pianists and conductors.

The label switching continued in 1984, with Levine doing Orff's *Carmina Burana* and Mendelssohn's *Midsummer Night's Dream* for DG, and symphonies by Dvořák and Tchaikovsky for RCA. Abbado kept pace by doing Tchaikovsky's Symphony no. 2 for CBS, the beginning of a full cycle, and on DG, Mahler's Symphony no. 7. What a year! There was another opera with Solti, Schoenberg's *Moses und Aron.* This is referred to in chapter 1, "Music Directors." The process continued in '85 and '86 with two new conductors in 1986 on CBS: Leonard Slatkin doing Bruch, and Michael Tilson Thomas recording Charles Ives.

The major effort in 1987 was the recording of Bach's *St. Matthew Passion* with Solti. This is a grand work with a large chorus and several soloists, and great solo parts for the orchestra musicians. Tales of this venture are in chapter 8, "Singers."

The following year saw Solti finishing up his Beethoven symphony cycle and Abbado working on his Tchaikovsky group, with Symphony no. 4 and *Romeo and Juliet.* Again we had someone new with whom to work: Leonard Bernstein. I mention this in chapter 5, "Guest Conductors."

Things never seemed to get into a strict pattern during these "glory" years, and maybe that is why we never got lax or bored. The usual recording dates were there in 1989: Solti, Abbado, Levine, and Tilson Thomas with Ives's Symphonies no. 1 and no. 4 on the new CBS label, Sony. We also worked with Neeme Järvi, a fine conductor from Estonia, who became music director of the Detroit Symphony Orchestra and later of the New Jersey Symphony.

His label was Chandos, and a change was made. The concerts were recorded live and the CD was put together from the tapes of the concerts. This was soon to be the way many companies operated, instead of having special recording sessions. At this time we made two CDs, Franz Schmidt's Symphony no. 2 and Mussorgsky's *Pictures at an Exhibition*, with Scriabin's *Poem of Ecstasy.* In another year we did two more CDs with Järvi, the Schmidt Symphony no. 3 and Kodály's *Háry János* suite, *Peacock Variations*, and *Dances of Galánta.*

Mentioning Järvi's CD of Mussorgsky's *Pictures* brings to mind that five recordings were made of that work during my years in the orchestra. An equal number were made of Mahler's Symphony no. 1 and Tchaikovsky's Symphony no. 5. On the "four times" list are Bartók's Concerto for orchestra, Beethoven's Symphony no. 5, Berlioz's *Symphonie fantastique*, Brahms's Symphony no. 1, Brahms's Symphony no. 4, Tchaikovsky's *Romeo and Juliet Overture*, and his Symphony no. 6. To hear the same orchestra playing each work four or five times is an education in the plusses and minuses of each recording company. It is also fascinating to hear the piece of music interpreted so differently by each conductor. But most of all, it is a testimonial to the flexibility and artistry of the Chicago Symphony Orchestra in achieving the musical adjustments needed for different performances of the same music.

The Gunther Wand disaster of 1989 is discussed in chapter 5, "Guest Conductors." Fortunately we only had to deal with him once in a recording venue, with the Brahms First Symphony for RCA.

The years 1990 through 1993 saw the largest number of annual recordings that the orchestra had ever done. This was because Sir Georg Solti was soon to retire as music director and Decca wanted to "make hay" while the sun still shone. And Daniel Barenboim was soon to enter as successor to Solti, so his new French company, Erato, wanted to get its foot in the door. In addition, Claudio Abbado continued his Tchaikovsky symphony cycle for Sony, and James Levine, still active at Ravinia, recorded with us.

In January of 1990, Sir Georg scheduled four concerts of the music of Debussy: *The Nocturnes, La mer,* and *Prelude to the Afternoon of a Faun*. But it was a tense time. The concerts of Debussy, being recorded live, were alternated over a two-week period with three programs of the Bach b minor Mass, which was also being recorded live. To compound the tension, there were separate recording sessions thrown in, between rehearsals and concerts, for the Bartók Divertimento for strings and the Beethoven Symphony no. 2.

We had previously recorded, in earlier years, *La mer* and the *Faun*, but this was the first time for the *Nocturnes*. Solti was just getting into the live recording mode and was a bit anxious. By the fourth night of this program Decca apparently didn't yet have a usable take of the opening of "Clouds," the first of the three *Nocturnes*. Solti requested us to be diligent so we could be certain to "get it" at this concert. We didn't know why he was so nervous, as there was always a re-take session scheduled for after the concert.

Nevertheless, we started the "Clouds," soft clarinet and oboe expressionism. It was a chilly January in Chicago. Audience members had colds and the flu. There were a number of coughs and sneezes. Sir Georg was livid. After maybe twelve measures he stopped the concert. He turned to the audience. He didn't quite scream, but his ire was evident. He told them to be quiet, or leave the auditorium and cough out in the lobby. We were shocked. After all, the audience had bought tickets to a *concert*, not to a recording session. This was not the usual Solti manner. Nerves do tell.

In any case, we started again. I do not remember if the audience was quiet or not, or if we had a re-take session after the concert. However, the recording is absolutely beautiful, including the *Faun* and *La Mer.* There were no difficulties with the alternating b minor Mass, which had a wonderful group of soloists, including Anne Sofie van Otter. Later that year, Solti recorded live a fine version of Shostakovich's Tenth Symphony, although I must admit a preference for the seductive one from a concert done in 1966 by Leopold Stokowski and issued on the Chicago Symphony Archives label.

In chapter 3, "Touring the World," I relate the stories of our trip to Russia in November of 1990. In Leningrad, as it was called then, we recorded Symphony no. 8 by Bruckner, and, later in the tour, did a live taping of Mahler's Symphony no. 5 at our concert in Vienna at the Musikverein. This was our second recording of this with Solti. In February Abbado added to his Tchaikovsky cycle with the Third Symphony and the *1812 Overture* for Sony. In addition there was Jimmy Levine on DG in July.

We had our first encounter with Erato Records in September of 1990, with Daniel Barenboim conducting. He began a Richard Strauss cycle with *Don Juan, Till Eulenspiegel,* and *Ein Heldenleben.* Also, he recorded the Symphony no. 1 by the CSO's composer-in-residence, John Corigliano. For a reason that we never understood, Erato hired some local, inexperienced engineer and producer to manage the sessions. The results are CDs that are mushy and muddy, with no clarity or personal tone of the orchestra or of any individual in it. It could be anybody playing.

Erato returned in 1991, with Barenboim recording a Ravel album including *Daphnis and Chloe* suite no. 2 and the *Rhapsodie espagnole,* Mahler's *Das Lied von der Erde, Don Quixote* by Richard Strauss with the orchestra's wonderful cellist John Sharp as soloist, and a CD of Wagner excerpts featuring soprano Deborah Polaski. Erato had slightly improved its act by this time, and this group of CDs is more honest in its reproduction of the orchestra sound than the earlier ones.

Over the years the orchestra had performed Ravel's *Daphnis and Chloe* music ninety-seven times with various conductors. It is always a challenge for the flutist, yet filled with rewards, because of the grand flute solo, probably the longest in the entire repertoire. This new Barenboim recording was our third. In 1964 we did it with Jean Martinon, and in 1987 with Sir Georg Solti on a Chicago Symphony Archives disc. It is interesting to hear these three versions because of the differences in each conductor's approach. Barenboim's tempos lean to the slower side, but the suavity and fulfillment of the musical lines is inspiring. I do like the flute solo best on this CD.

Pierre Boulez joined the parade by recording with us in December 1991, on Erato, a Schoenberg CD, *Variations for Orchestra*, and Debussy's *Pelléas et Mélisande*. With more label switching, a week later we worked with Boulez on DG, doing Bartók's *Wooden Prince* ballet and *Cantata profana*.

Another new label arrived in 1991, Koch. We did concerts with a young conductor, Andrew Schenck: the music of Samuel Barber, *Prayers of Kierkegaard* and *The Lovers*. These were issued on a CD and won a Grammy Award. More collaborations were planned between him and the orchestra, but he died in England less than a year later.

Levine continued on DG with Stravinsky, and Abbado on Sony with Tchaikovsky. Sir Georg had another big year with a Tippett CD, Bruckner's Symphony no. 2, plus four concerts in Chicago and New York of Verdi's opera *Otello*. These concerts and their live recording are referred to in chapter 8, "Singers," with particular comments on Luciano Pavarotti.

The Richard Strauss cycle on Erato continued in 1992 with Daniel Barenboim doing the *Alpine* symphony. He also recorded a Johann Strauss waltz album and the Concerto for orchestra by Lutoslawski. But his big item of the year was the Brahms *Requiem*, with Thomas Hampson, baritone. Solti continued his vocal extravaganzas by taping Haydn's *The Seasons*. Bruckner's Symphony no. 3 was added to Solti's cycle, along with a second recording of Berlioz's *Symphonie fantastique* and Liszt's *Les preludes*. Boulez was active now on DG with a Bartók album and the complete *Firebird* ballet by Stravinsky. Likewise active on DG was James Levine, recording Prokofiev's Symphony no. 5 and the Berg Violin Concerto, with Annie-Sophie Mutter.

Of the four grandest recording years, 1993 topped them all, with everybody doing everything! That should take care of that. More specifically, Solti did another recording of Haydn's *The Creation*. We threw together music of Liszt, Kodály, and Bartók for a Hungarian album, and got heavily into Stravinsky with the two symphonies, the complete *Petrouchka*, and *Jeu de cartes*. We heard later from witty English friends that Sir Georg took a six-month vacation to rest after this.

But we didn't. We continued with Boulez, recording the Bartók opera *Bluebeard's Castle* with Jessye Norman. And something new and fun was the making of the soundtrack for the new movie *Fantasia 2000*, conducted by James Levine on DG. We recorded heavily cut versions of Beethoven's Symphony no. 5 and Respighi's *The Pines of Rome*, for starters. Did you know that Beethoven's Fifth Symphony only takes seven minutes? These sessions were spread over three separate years, thrown in at the end of regular recording sessions. We never had contact with any film people, nor did we see the cartoons for which we were playing, except later in the theater.

Daniel Barenboim had a banner year of Erato recordings in 1993. First of all we did all four symphonies of Brahms. This made the orchestra look back on the years of recording and decide that we should be called the Brahms Orchestra as well as the Mahler Orchestra. We had made three complete sets of the symphonies, with Solti, Levine, and Barenboim, as well as additional CDs with single symphonies of other conductors. Further, we did three CDs of the *Requiem*, two of the violin concerto, and five of the two piano concerti.

Continuing with Barenboim, we recorded the Prokofiev No. 2 and Mendelssohn violin concerti with Itzhak Perlman, Rimsky-Korsakov's *Scheherazade* (our third recording), and another Wagner album. One Wagner CD was issued on Erato, the other two eventually on Teldec. Some smaller works were added to fill out the four-symphony set, Brahms's Haydn Variations and overtures.

But the most amazing of events, looking back on that year, was the taping of two more large choral works, with Barenboim, to join Brahms's *German Requiem*, which we had taped in 1992. These were the Verdi *Requiem* and Beethoven's *Missa solemnis*. This achievement speaks so highly of the wonderful Chicago Symphony Chorus, which had to prepare and perform all of that music, in addition to working at their regular jobs.

The reasoning behind all of Daniel Barenboim's recording in 1993 became clear in 1994. I don't remember any announcement, or explanation from the management, but the company that came to Orchestra Hall to record in 1994 was no longer Erato, but Teldec, a German concern. Erato needed to use up its contract with Barenboim, we surmised, thus the efforts of 1993. The producer and engineer used by Teldec on each visit to us were great improvements over those from Erato. Our playbacks, and later the CDs, actually sounded somewhat like us.

We were in a lazy heaven in 1994, with a light year in front of the microphone. Barenboim directed some concerti with violinist Perlman and cellist Yo-Yo Ma, and a Schoenberg orchestral album. DG worked with Boulez again, doing the *Miraculous Mandarin* by Bartók.

We taped more background music with James Levine for *Fantasia 2000* in 1995, the Elgar *Enigma Variations*. Both Barenboim and Boulez had a large amount of recording, "Danny" doing Tchaikovsky's Symphonies nos. 4 and 5, *Romeo and Juliet*, the *1812 Overture*, Berlioz's *Symphonie fantastique*, an African music CD, and a contemporary recording of Berio, Takemitsu, and Carter. Boulez had his first outing with Mahler and us by recording the Symphony no. 9, and a Scriabin taping, with *Prometheus*, the *Poem of Ecstasy*, and the piano concerto.

Solti continued to do big items, this year another complete opera, Wagner's *Die Meistersinger*, with Ben Heppner, Rene Pape, José van Dam, and Karita Mattila. Altogether, we recorded six complete operas with Solti. Has any other symphony orchestra done so many operas and recorded them? Don't say Vienna, because the Vienna Philharmonic is the opera orchestra of the Vienna State Opera. They give only a few symphonic concerts. Surprise?

But Solti wasn't finished for 1995, as he also did two Bruckner symphonies, no. 1 and no. 0, and Shostakovich's Symphony no. 13, *Babi Yar*. The latter is a huge, seventy-four-minute work with a bass soloist, a chorus, and a narrator, Sir Anthony Hopkins on this recording. This symphony is not often played, perhaps because of the difficulty in putting it all together. It also is not the most ear-grabbing experience, and yet, listening to the recording with the text available to read, it can be a fascinating historical document. The poems, by Yevgeny Yevtushenko, concern the Russian revolutions of 1905 and 1917 and their cruelty and persecution; Yevtushenko was aiming to become a spokesman for the post-Stalin generation of young Russians.

We had a definite falling off of recording dates in 1996, with Barenboim only taping two violin concerti and the Brahms Double Concerto, and Solti doing none. With Boulez we did an album of Varese featuring *Arcana*, and another of Strauss's *Also sprach Zarathustra* coupled with Mahler's *Totenfeier*. Levine did the final round of *Fantasia 2000* with us, Stravinsky's *Firebird*.

No one was yet happy with the acoustics of Orchestra Hall. Since the hall was good for recitals and small chamber music groups, there were those who felt that it was time to build an entirely new orchestra hall elsewhere and leave the current space for the smaller concerts. Opposing them were those who thought that the old hall should be done over again. Opinion number two won out. In the spring of 1997 work was begun on a complete renovation. The orchestra, therefore, had to do the concerts from May onward in another venue, Medinah Temple, our recording home for a few years.

At that time two concerts were taped by Teldec and issued as CDs. One was an exciting album of music by Manuel de Falla: *The Three-Cornered Hat* with Jennifer Larmore, mezzo-soprano, and *Nights in the Gardens of Spain* with Barenboim at the piano, conducted by Placido Domingo. The second was music of Bernstein and Gershwin. Barenboim made only one other CD with us that year, the Brahms Violin Concerto, with soloist Vengerov. Levine had moved on to the Metropolitan Opera, so we didn't see him. Boulez had no recording with us in 1997, but Solti was again in evidence with a live taping of Symphony no. 15 by Shostakovich, with a Mussorgsky filler.

The orchestra left on a European tour at the end of May, as the work continued on the hall. We returned in June in time to do the summer Ravinia Festival. Following a vacation, the '98–'99 season opened on September 25. The "new" hall does have a different look, with some audience seating behind the orchestra, as is the current vogue. The ambiance in the space has been improved, but there are three severe negatives. The sound in the auditorium varies a great deal depending on where one sits. The orchestra players cannot hear one another properly. And the front of the stage does not project the sound into the hall as much as the rear does. So the first violins and a soloist are at a big disadvantage. The feeling soon spread that it would have been better to have built a new auditorium elsewhere. These discussions are ongoing.

After his success with Mahler's Ninth Symphony, Boulez recorded Mahler's First Symphony in 1998. Barenboim did Tchaikovsky's Symphony no. 6 in Chicago, and then on tour in Cologne we recorded a live performance of Mahler's Symphony no. 5. Barenboim had joined the pack of Chicago-Mahlerites.

The first recording that I made with the Chicago Symphony orchestra was during my first season, '57–'58: the Brahms Piano Concerto no. 2, Fritz Reiner conducting, with pianist Emil Gilels. The final recording I made was on January 6 and 8, 1999, my forty-second and last season with the orchestra. It was the third Wagner CD with Barenboim: the *Rienzi* overture, the prelude and Good Friday music from *Parsifal*, the prelude to act 3 of *Tannhäuser*, excerpts from *Die Meistersinger*, and the *Siegfried* idyll.

I am gratified to have been a part of the history of the Chicago Symphony Orchestra during those forty-two peak years. We received many rewards and awards. With Sir Georg Solti we accrued twenty-four Grammy Awards. Sir Georg overall has won thirty Grammys, more than any other individual. We received two more awards with Pierre Boulez, current principal guest conductor, plus one for the Samuel Barber album conducted by Andrew Schenck.

In covering the years of recordings I have discussed the repertoire, the conductors, and the concert halls, but some of the fine record producers should also be mentioned. During the Reiner/RCA days there was Richard Mohr, whom I consider to be the most knowledgeable, caring, and musically sincere of all the producers I have ever worked with. Also with RCA were Paul Goodman and Howard Scott. Howard later went over to CBS. EMI/Angel used the intelligent and flexible Peter Andry, and at other times Richard Jones. We definitely appreciated Gunther Breest doing our earlier DG recordings, for he was a man with many of the qualities of Richard Mohr. He later moved into a governing position at the headquarters of DG. Recording for Decca/London, we first worked with James Mallinson. He was quick and bright, and seemed to enjoy our performances, so we got along very well. He did some assignments for Sony, too, coming to Chicago to record the Tchaikovsky symphonies with Claudio Abbado. Later from Decca/London we had Michael Haas. Like all of these gentlemen, he had knowledge of music and of the electronics involved in the recording process, as well as wit and civility.

This group of producers seemed to have been well trained musically and in their recording work. For these reasons, they could hear the difference in the tone quality of a variety of orchestras. They considered it their job to pick up that sound from each group. That's why the Philadelphia Orchestra was itself, the Berlin Philharmonic was itself, the Chicago Symphony was itself, etc.

This aim was gradually corrupted by the introduction of more and more sophisticated electronic equipment, more "toys," which enabled the engineers to become stars, to manufacture any sound that they desired instead of reproducing that which was being played. At some point in the '80s it became impossible to tell which orchestra was playing on a recording. Everything sounded the same because of the interference of the staff. Remember the days of one microphone suspended above the orchestra? Now they used thirty or forty spread all over the stage and out into the hall. Someone must have cried "foul," or the bosses finally listened to our complaints, because in the late 1980s and into the 1990s the stardom of the engineers and producers was put in check. They got back to reproducing what had been performed. In any case, every life and career has a flow upward and an ebb downward. We can only put on our French berets, shrug, and say, "C'est la vie."

It is not worth worrying about now, since the recording industry is going through a very bad period. Everything has been recorded several times, and everyone has already bought it. There is almost no recording of orchestral works being done at this time. When I think of the three hundred LPs and CDs with which I was involved, I can only repeat, "It helps to be in the right place at the right time."

11

Solo Dates

With the Chicago Symphony Orchestra

*E*ach season a few members of the Chicago Symphony played concerti with the orchestra. In my forty-two years in the group I was soloist in 123 concerts with twenty-eight different conductors, at Orchestra Hall, at the Ravinia Festival, and on tour. My first solo date with the orchestra was on November 4 and 5, 1960, in the Bach Suite in b minor with Fritz Reiner conducting. In 1998 I made my last appearances, on December 17, 18, 19, and 20. The work was the Nielsen Concerto for flute, with Daniel Barenboim as conductor.

The work I played the most times with the Chicago Symphony was the Mozart Concerto for flute and harp, with Edward Druzinsky, harpist. We gave thirteen performances with many conductors, including Fritz Reiner, Walter Hendl, Seiji Ozawa, and Irwin Hoffman. Alone, I was almost as prolific, performing the Concerto no. 2 for Flute in D Major by Mozart twelve times, conducted by Sir Georg Solti and James Levine, among others. The Mozart Concerto no. 1 for Flute in G Major I did eight times, with directors Mark Wigglesworth and the inspiring Rafael Kubelik.

Another often-performed piece was the Frank Martin Concerto for seven winds. On a tour in 1966 with Jean Martinon conducting, we played it in southern and eastern states, ending up at Carnegie Hall, for a total of twenty performances of the work. We then recorded it with Martinon for RCA. Later, in 1992, Erich Leinsdorf conducted it in four concerts.

All in all, I performed twenty-nine different solo works with the Chicago Symphony Orchestra. And such a variety! Tons of Bach, Telemann, and Vivaldi. Mozart has already been mentioned, leading to more Romantic endeavors like Chaminade and Bloch. There were modern works with a Romantic bent, like those of Griffes, Hanson, Nielsen, Martinu, and Martin. Some slightly farther-out composers were Foss, Barber, Diamond, Ghedini, Gould, and Gesensway. Only a couple got out of hand, or ear: van Vlijmen and Berio. But with a considered approach I think that we made them listenable. For me, the most exciting, rewarding, and touching concerto event was the Morton Gould Concerto for flute and orchestra, in 1985.

When I went to California in 1970 to play in the Carmel Bach Festival I met a wonderful lady, Katherine Lewis. She was in her seventies at that time. We became good friends. She even visited Chicago on occasion, once bringing my opera protagonist, Bill Samuel. Having lived in Chicago in the '30s with her artist husband, Herbert Lewis, Katie was a big fan of the Chicago Symphony Orchestra and of music in general.

She was pleased to have met me in these later years of her life, and in 1980 offered to commission a flute concerto for me. In deciding which composer to approach, I remembered the fine relationship I had with Morton Gould in the '60s, when he conducted and recorded in Chicago. I had even seen him a few times socially in New York. I discussed this with orchestra manager John Edwards, who liked the idea.

Morton Gould had been trapped early in his career by being too successful with a lighter vein of music, sometimes to the point that his more serious work was not accepted. I knew that he was a very talented man, frustrated by his own reputation. He accepted the commission immediately.

On a visit to New York I met with him to get his ideas about a concerto. I was appalled. He said that he had thought out six cute little movements with a small orchestra. I replied, quite strongly, "NO!" I said that I wanted a powerful, dramatic, musically important, expressive pylon of a concerto. I asked him to utilize his grand musical instincts. He looked quite surprised, but then extremely pleased. No one had ever asked that of him.

So he set to work. He kept me posted on developments and often sent me sections of the concerto that he had finished. He also called Katie in Carmel and kept her up to date on what was happening. This made her very happy.

Gould worked for two years on the concerto, making it a four-movement opus. Near the end of that period he sent me the final movement. I played it through a few times. It was a brisk, lighter movement than the other three. I felt that it needed a section to bring in the deeper moods of the previous movements in order to tie the whole work together. I suggested this to Morton.

What he did was genius. He built up the fourth movement to a stirring climax and then made a cut-off, a grand pause. It then continued, softly, tenderly, with a gentle orchestration that had the flute weaving in and out of the texture. This gradually built up, slowly at first and then with more vehemence, to an exciting coda that ripped off the ceiling. That change of mood had really done it.

Solti agreed to conduct the premiere, which was set for April 18, 19, and 20, 1985. Morton Gould came to town for the rehearsals to hear if he should be making any changes. He did make a few in the orchestration and a couple in the flute part. Especially important was his re-thinking of the last note of the solo. It is a high D, that is, three octaves and a note above middle C on the piano. It is an achievement just to produce this pitch without sounding edgy and ugly. He had made it even worse by writing it to be flutter-tongued, which means with a quivering of the tongue in the mouth, which makes the note sound shrill and quaking. After one rehearsal, he took out the flutter-tonguing, for which I was very grateful. Unfortunately, Gould's music publisher, G. Schirmer, didn't check for any changes that he had made and published the concerto in its original, unfinished state. Publishers rarely re-do an edition once it has gone on the market, but I do have the finished version of the concerto if someone would like to contact me.

Katie was coming to Chicago to hear the premiere. She bought a new wardrobe, got her airplane and hotel reservations, and spoke to me on the phone with joyful expectancy. Two weeks before the date she had a stroke and died within two days. I was devastated. By a stunt of fate, again, the slow movement of the concerto is an Elegy with Variations. An elegy is music that you play in memory of one who has died. It even has a reference to the *Dies Irae*. This was another stunt of fate.

When we came to that movement I almost had to stop. It was very difficult to continue playing. All I could think about was Katie. Over the next few years I gave six more performances of this concerto with other orchestras. The same crush of feelings came to me in that second movement. Katie had been a wonderful person. I liked her and appreciated her. With the concerto commission she established her own memorial.

When she and her artist husband, Herbert Lewis, lived in Chicago in the '30s, he did an Art Deco–style sketch of the Chicago Symphony from the gallery in Orchestra Hall. As a study he made a watercolor painting of the sketch, 1½ ft. by 2 ft., that Katie gave to me in 1983, which I have on my wall. In the 1940s, after he and Katie had moved to California, he did a huge oil painting of this for Angie Machado's mansion in Carmel. It was the full realization of the Chicago Symphony sketch. The Chicago Symphony management liked it so much that they used it as a program cover during the '88–'89 season. I was thrilled. This was a further memorial to Katie.

I had many concerto dates with the CSO after the Gould, mainly Mozart concerti with three different conductors. But in 1998, when I was preparing to leave the orchestra, the management and Barenboim asked me to stay another year to give them time to find a replacement. They threw in the idea of Barenboim and me performing the Nielsen Concerto. I had done it years earlier, with Irwin Hoffman conducting, but welcomed the chance for one final appearance as soloist. We did four performances. To me, it was a fitting preamble to my departure in June of 1999.

Outside of the Chicago Symphony Orchestra

Over the years, I did eighty-one solo performances with orchestras other than the Chicago Symphony. When they are combined with the 123 dates with the CSO, we have a respectable number of 204. A full-time solo artist would have had more, of course, but would not have been dealing with the orchestra schedule, teaching, and other events.

Number-wise, the Mozart Flute and Harp Concerto leads the pack: thirteen performances with the CSO and thirty-five elsewhere, making forty-eight performances of that work. Most of these were with harpist Edward Druzinsky, but I did several more with five other harpists. In the list of cities are Charlotte, Chattanooga, Greenville, Madison, Carmel, Erie, Kansas City, Washington, D.C., Santa Fe, Dubuque, and Cedar Rapids, to name a few.

At times, it felt like Druzinsky and I were building a career on the Flute and Harp Concerto. When we were nearing a new solo date, we agreed that we should rehearse. After performance number fifteen the rehearsal seemed pointless, since we both knew the music and each other's playing. We often cut the rehearsal short and had an earlier vodka martini than we might have had.

So we would get to the new orchestra, have a rehearsal with that group, and arrive on stage for the concert. Sometimes some little goof would occur: wrong pedal pushed, not enough breath taken in, or a memory lapse. But we were pros. We collected ourselves and went on to finish in the usual blaze of approval. We bowed and walked off the stage.

We immediately turned to each other while waiting to go out for a curtain call and said, "Next time we *have* to rehearse." Of course, the "next time" was usually the same routine as "this time." It became our warm, personal, standing joke.

The Mozart Concerto in D Major was big for me, too, with twelve performances in Chicago and fourteen in other cities, like Seattle, Lynchburg, Victoria, Biloxi, Rockford, Carmel, Topeka, and Webster. The Telemann Suite in a minor had a good run of seven dates. Even a new work like the Morton Gould Concerto was performed in five locales outside of Chicago —Monterey, Salinas, Carmel, Kalamazoo, and Kansas City. I did concerto dates with other works by Griffes, Hanson, Nielsen, Grier, Bach, Chaminade, Poulenc, and Bach. Like all large cities, Chicago is surrounded by suburban communities, each with its own symphony orchestra. I certainly hit all of those in the area, some more than once, like Evanston, Gary, Wilmette, Highland Park, Woodstock, Aurora, Benton Harbor, Oak Park, Elmhurst, etc.

Other solo dates were flute recitals, often given in conjunction with a master class at a university. I won't even try to count the number of those. You name the state, I was probably there. Doing a recital on these occasions could be problematic, because sometimes I had to work with a pianist who did not know my musical approach, and vice versa. In two rehearsals only, we had to put together a full program. I remember a couple of disasters, one in Portland, Oregon, and another in Orlando, Florida. But the good ones come to mind too, like those in Louisville, New York City, and Newcastle, Australia. I suppose it does even out. Well, maybe.

The Chamber Music Scene

For twelve years in my Chicago Symphony history there existed a chamber music ensemble composed of the nine first-chair people, except for the oboe, called the Chicago Symphony Chamber Players. We had occasionally performed with each other in various-sized groups but in 1978 we banded together as a unit. Our repertoire consisted of duets to nonets, strings or winds, or mixed. We constantly added to our list of music with much help from our bassoonist, Willard Elliot, who made several arrangements for us. One in particular, which we played many times, was called Scriabiniana for nine instruments, based on nine piano preludes of Scriabin.

A New York composer, Lee Hoiby, composer of the opera *Summer and Smoke*, wrote a new work for our group, Ten Variations on a Schubert *Ländler* for nine instruments. Lee dedicated it to me since we were friends from years ago, when we were both students at the Curtis Institute of Music. At that time, for my graduation recital in 1951, he composed the Pastorale Dances for flute and piano, which he later arranged with an orchestra accompaniment.

We always faced the problem of trying to book our chamber music dates around the CSO schedule. Unfortunately, we had to refuse many offers. In '78 and '79 we were fine, with concerts in Birmingham, Detroit, and Waukegan, at the Ravinia Festival, and at the University of Illinois in Chicago and in Champaign-Urbana. Things started to swing in 1980 with a large concert at Orchestra Hall in Chicago, visits again to the two University of Illinois campuses, and performances in Palm Beach, Florida, and at the University of Maryland, Harper College, and the Art Institute Series in Chicago. Over the next few years, performance dates abounded, in places including, to mention only a few, La Jolla, San Francisco, Detroit, Toronto, Kansas City, Melbourne, Florida, and Alice Tully Hall in New York City. Since we didn't wish to play the same music at every concert, each date required several hours of rehearsal. Again, trying to fit those rehearsals in with the orchestra routine, our teaching agenda, and personal solo engagements became a marathon. How did we do it? It is amazing to realize that we didn't even think about it. We loved doing it, so we just did it. Maybe musicians are neurotics, but happy neurotics.

We had two biggies for our diaries in 1989. They were both special, but in very different ways. From June 5 to 19 we gave chamber concerts in Japan: four in Tokyo and one each in Matsuyama, Osaka, Setuda, and Nagoya. The audience response was remarkable, as were the reviews: "Supreme artistry," "Impeccably able to play anything," "What a fantastic evening!"

The other event that we were anticipating was a concert in San Francisco, on October 17, 1989. Does that date ring a bell? We got to the hall, Herbst Theatre, at 4 PM for a rehearsal. At 5 PM the building started to tremble, just a little at first, and then the big earthquake hit us. All the lights went out, the stage rocked from side to side, and the walls cracked as the plaster cornices were thrown off onto the floor. It felt like a giant had picked up the building and was shaking it violently. The stagehands rushed onto stage and told us to join hands, as it was pitch dark, and they would lead us out of the building.

An adjacent park was filling up with the outpouring of people from the Opera House next door. We mingled and exchanged stories of anxiety and joy. Forty-five minutes passed before we could re-enter the building to pick up our instruments. We were told to do it as fast as possible. I must admit that I walked around inside for a few moments, looking at all of the damage: piles of plaster lying about, part of the ceiling torn out, broken windows, cracked marble floors. I sneaked out with a piece of plaster that had fallen from an ornate molding. I use it as an "item" on the coffee table in my living room.

The concert, of course, was canceled. We walked back to the hotel, which now had no electricity. Each room had been fitted with a gas lantern. The hotel did try to make us feel comfortable. Drinks were free in the bar, and some snacks were passed around to take the place of the dinner that was not being served. The staff and customers were all in a warm, friendly mood, perhaps to cover up for the tension of a few hours earlier.

Going to my room later, when the sun had gone down, I looked out the window. There was still no electricity, so there were no streetlights or building illumination. Only an occasional car drove through the street. It was a black, frightening landscape. I looked across the bay, to Oakland. A double-deck viaduct had collapsed there, killing some people and trapping others. I could see it from my room. It was eerie and heart-wrenching.

The next day the members of our group made their way to the airport, trying to get flights back to Chicago. Some of them spent many hours waiting. I had the week off, so I drove down to Carmel to visit friends. Damage was evident all along the highway, through San Jose and Santa Cruz and into Monterey-Carmel. It was a wake-up experience, making me realize how minimal we are compared to the real powers of the universe.

The concert association that had booked us into San Francisco contacted us soon after. They asked us to give them another date to return to San Francisco and perform the concert. I spoke to the group, mentioning that earthquakes don't happen very often. San Francisco had now had an earthquake and it was safe for many years. But the vote went five to four not to return.

The last year of the Chicago Symphony Chamber Players as an organized unit was 1990. We still did chamber music concerts, often with each other, but I believe we all felt that it was time to move on to achieve some diversity after our twelve-year "marriage." Dale Clevenger, French horn, turned to orchestra conducting and eventually took over a suburban ensemble, the Elmhurst Symphony, in his spare time. Concertmaster Samuel Magad presided over and played in the Chicago Symphony String Quartet, and became the music director of the Northbrook Symphony Orchestra. Clarinetist Larry Combs formed his own group, not exclusively composed of CSO members, the Chicago Symphony Chamber Players.

I turned to playing more recitals, including three in New York City at the Manhattan School of Music, Powell Flutes, and Town Hall. I also worked with two chamber groups, the Lydian Trio and Trio Concertante. The latter was very busy over many years, with my good friend the oboist Wayne Rapier and a variety of pianists. Our concert dates included Baltimore, Philadelphia, Oberlin, Chicago, and New York City. In addition, I taped five CDs of flute and piano music between 1994 and 2000 for Boston Records.

The plethora of outside recital and chamber music engagements for some of the Chicago Symphony members might not have happened except for the notoriety of the orchestra. Nevertheless, our acclaimed solo appearances in a host of other cities did contribute to the reputation of the orchestra in the '80s and '90s, even though our management on occasion was reluctant to give us the time off to accept these dates. I attempted to make the point that these engagements were a positive thing for the orchestra's name, plus, when we returned, it was with renewed interest after the time away.

Music Publications

Getting into another solo dates endeavor brings up the pleasure I derived from having some of my music arrangements issued by publishers. Consolidated Music Publishers, who have a series called Music for Millions, first approached me. Mine is volume 48, called *Easy Original Flute Solos*. It consists of some of the easier flute pieces and several orchestral excerpts with a piano accompaniment added. That came out in 1967 and is still on the market.

In reading a biography of Claude Debussy many years ago, I came across mention of a work that he had written in 1900 called *Chansons de Bilitis* (not the songs). It was for two flutes, two harps, a celesta, and a narrator, set to poems by Pierre Louys. Debussy put this aside and it was never published. He later used some of the themes in his *Six epigraphes antiques*. I had never seen this music, obviously, but one day, while on tour in Brussels, I browsed through an out-of-the-way music store and found a photocopy of a handwritten version, completed for the instruments by Pierre

Boulez. Naturally, I bought it and performed it the next year in Chicago at an Orchestra Hall chamber music concert.

I had a wonderful, rich-voiced vocal coach, Lola Rand, do the narration of the poems, which are quite risqué. We tried it in English but the sound was wrong for the definitive French music, so we went back to that language, with a translation in the program.

It is an extremely beautiful piece, so I made an arrangement for flute, piano, and narrator. Bourne published this in New York in 1979. I call it *Bilitis*, dropping the "Chansons" part so as to avoid confusion with the songs. Lola and I, and pianist Melody Lord, recorded it on one of my CDs. This seemed to create an interest in the music, as the market has since seen two other arrangements, each with its differences.

Mark Thomas and Gene Frank established a new publishing house in 1975 called Edu-Tainment Publishing. I was signed to do some editions, as were Paula Robeson, Doriot Dwyer, Bernhard Goldberg, and Mark Thomas. In each of three years they issued my editions of Andersen's Etudes for flute, Opp. 30, 33, and 63, and also brought out my performance version of the Concertino by Chaminade, a flute staple.

In 1978 some trouble was brewing. The company was not going to last long. Just at this time they were about to issue my flute and piano arrangement of the Franck Sonata in A Major, originally for violin. A host of copies were printed, but the company was soon gone. Gene Frank transferred to each of us the copyright on our editions. He also sent to me the multiple copies of the Franck Sonata, which he had in the storeroom. The other music he sold to some dealers, wholesale and retail, and that is where we didn't luck out, as we never got any royalties from the music in the hands of private businesses.

My next music came out in 1982 from Southern Music Company, an edition for flute and piano of the Mozart Andante in C Major with my original cadenza. This has been available for over twenty years and still has good sales in the United States and England.

Publisher Carl Fischer got onto me in 1984 to do a compilation of medium-difficulty flute and piano music. They called the edition *Solos for Flute: 36 Repertoire Pieces*. It's still available. During the intervening years, I did several other arrangements. One is of *Afternoon of a Faun*, by Debussy, for flute and piano. Flutists who perform this version say it's the best of the many arrangements on the market. Melody Lord and I recorded this. It is available on two of the Boston label CDs.

I became "attached" to the Theodore Presser Company in 1999 with their issuance of my edition of the Beethoven Romance in F, Op. 50. This violin piece works well for the flute, as can be heard on another of my Boston label CDs. In the year 2000, Presser suggested I make an arrangement for solo flute of a Bach unaccompanied cello suite. I chose no. 4 in E Flat as the best one for the flute, as there are fewer double stops to work around than in some of the other suites. I recorded four of the six movements on the Boston label the same year as publication, in 2000.

Presser issued another arrangement of mine in 2001, the Romance for violin, Op. 11, by Dvořák. I made a small cut in the middle so that a flute can more easily reach the climax around bar 83. My joke is that Dvořák spoke to me a week before he died and told me how much he liked it! Presser and I continue to talk about possible new arrangements and editions. I have considered "rescuing" the Oboe Concerto of Richard Strauss with a version for the flute, but the seventy-year copyright law is a problem, as the concerto was written in 1945. We will see.

My latest publisher contact is Progress Press in Evanston, Ill. They have issued my three Andersen etude books (which were formerly with Edu-Tainment), my arrangement of Debussy's *Afternoon of a Faun*, and my edition of the Franck Sonata.

I hope that this chapter, in combination with the next one, "Outside Jobs," gives a clear idea of the arduous schedule that we maintained both in and out of the Chicago Symphony. It is also meant to show the great variety of musical endeavors in which we were involved. The life was definitely not a 9-to-5 job with the same routines each day. Granted, it did take a lot of time and a great deal of direction. But it was worth it, exciting and rewarding.

12

Outside Jobs

*I*n addition to executing the Symphony schedule, the musicians often accepted unrelated musical dates. These might be solo, chamber music, or recital performances, and often master classes and instrumental teaching. We called them outside jobs. They had to be arranged around the Symphony agenda.

The schedule for the Chicago Symphony Orchestra varied over the years, but was basically eight services per week. This could mean four rehearsals and four concerts, or five and three, or three and five. Occasionally a ninth service was added, but it had to be made up later with a seven-service week. To people not "in the know," this schedule didn't seem especially busy.

However, recording sessions were added every few weeks during the good times. These would be three-, six-, or nine-hour episodes, using up extra time during a regular eight-service week. Also, at one time we had a TV show called *Music in Chicago*. This was taped above and beyond the regular schedule, sometimes in a free evening, or maybe on a day off, like Sunday, in which case we had a seven-day week. Many of those tapes are now available on videotape and DVD from Video Artists International. Famous conductors abounded: Leopold Stokowski, Fritz Reiner, George Szell, Paul Hindemith, Sir Georg Solti, Pierre Monteux, Charles Münch, Sir Thomas Beecham, etc. It was exhilarating, but it did overfill the schedule.

Affecting mainly the first-chair players, but not entirely, was the Civic Orchestra of Chicago. This is a high-caliber training ensemble supported by the Chicago Symphony, with talented younger performers who had won nationwide auditions. Every week the principal player of each section of the CSO would coach that section from the Civic Orchestra in orchestral music and disciplines. That was another two hours gone. However, it was rewarding to be working with the fine talent. Many of the Symphony conductors led the Civic in rehearsals, and sometimes in concerts.

A majority of Symphony members also did instrumental teaching, either privately or in connection with a college, maybe both. I taught at DePaul University for thirty-five years, not just flute, but chamber music and flute master classes, and later at Roosevelt University. I also did a fair amount of private teaching, often to students from out of town who wanted a new idea, or those preparing for a recital or an audition. In some summers, I gave a week of master classes at DePaul with flutists from all across the country, and sometimes Europe and Japan. I always gave a flute recital during that week. Five of these were taped by Boston Records and issued as CDs.

All of these performances, in recitals, on TV, on recordings, and at the Orchestra concerts, required private practice. Even a piece that we had played before needed reviewing, and of course a new work had to be studied from scratch. We could not go to rehearsals and make mistakes. This was a demand of being in the Chicago Symphony, as well as of our own pride. We then rehearsed it to put it together as a unit. Plus, it is not enough just to play music several hours a week. One has to practice meticulously to keep a high level of technical and tonal control on the instrument. Dig out the etudes, the scales, the thirds, the long tones. This we called maintenance.

There were extra jobs around town that we took part in: maybe a ballet, or a small symphony concert, or whatever. Also, at one time, Chicago was a major city for the taping of TV commercials. We were often hired as part of the studio musical group for the background music. This paid extremely well and sometimes continued in residuals for a few years, when the commercial was repeated. I remember doing a commercial for Hallmark cards that went on with the residuals for several years.

Many of the Symphony members were hired to give master classes outside of Chicago, at universities, festivals, and music clubs. I did over a hundred of these, in Australia, Canada, Japan, the Netherlands, and Puerto Rico, as well as throughout the United States. Locales included the Juilliard and Manhattan Schools in New York City, the San Francisco Conservatory, Indiana University, the University of Texas, the University of Houston, Rice University, the New World Symphony in Florida, Sydney,

Australia (three times!), the Tanglewood Festival in Massachusetts, etc. Many of these dates included a flute recital. On occasion, when the orchestra was on tour, a university in a concert city would schedule one or several of us for a master class. This made the tours all the more tiring. Still, we didn't say no. I've never been sure why we accepted these engagements. Was it for the money, or our egos? Maybe both, but it was also rewarding dealing with the talent that I coached all over the world, even when it added to the strain of the job.

Each summer there are music festivals that draw musicians from around the world to perform in solo, chamber music, and orchestra concerts. It can be a wonderful experience for the players, as they interact with a new group of artists, different from those of their normal winter season. Then the regular job becomes revitalized when they return to it in the autumn. All in all, a very good idea.

My first experience with a summer event was in 1957. I was leaving my post in the Kansas City Philharmonic, on my way to the Chicago Symphony, so my summer was free. How happy I was to be invited to play the premiere season of the Santa Fe Opera. I came to know and love Santa Fe and return every few years just to visit. I was invited back to play future Opera seasons but was never able to get a summer free from the Chicago Symphony's Ravinia season. In the early '60s I bought three acres of sagebrush south of Santa Fe, on Rodeo Road. The city then proceeded to expand in that direction. If I had been smarter, or richer, I would have bought twenty acres. When I sold the land around 1980, the price was outrageous. I almost felt guilty.

John Crosby founded the opera company. His father, in the sugar business, owned a great deal of land just north of Santa Fe. John was an opera lover and decided to try his hand in that field. He was nothing but a success. He conducted at least one opera each summer, usually by Richard Strauss, his favorite composer. The first year it was *Ariadne auf Naxos*. Other operas for the first season were *Madama Butterfly, Così fan tutte, The Barber of Seville, The Tower,* by the American Marvin David Levy, and *The Rake's Progress,* by Igor Stravinsky. Stravinsky was present and coached the rehearsals, with Robert Craft conducting the orchestra. Stravinsky conducted the final rehearsal and all of the performances. What a thrill to be involved in this new venture.

We had a marvelous orchestra. A few of us banded together and formed a chamber music group, performing in downtown Santa Fe, at the Art Gallery, and in a strange and eerie place that was very secretive, even twenty-two years after World War II. This was Los Alamos, where the atom bomb had been perfected.

We were driven up through the hills, with astonishing vistas, to the iron gates, where military personnel scrutinized us at length. After gaining admittance, we performed a program in a school auditorium: C. P. E. Bach's Sonata in a minor for solo flute, Debussy's Sonata for flute, viola, and harp, and Françaix's Quintet for winds. Afterward there was a gracious party given by some high figure in the installation. We had the impression that the extremely intelligent people involved in the project rarely got out into the world. They seemed so happy to see us, to speak with us.

John Crosby also directed the orchestra for a concert in which I played the Mozart Concerto for flute and harp, with harpist Lee Swinson. All in all, a great summer! The Santa Fe Opera has since expanded considerably, with two different additions to the theater. A roof was installed, as too many operas had been rained out, but the sides are still open to give a view of the spectacular scenery. One year, on a visit, I went to see *Elektra*. Halfway through the opera we were hit by a mammoth lightning storm. Everyone agreed that it had been an "Elektrafying" performance!

In 1963 I played the Festival Casals in Puerto Rico. The usual flutist for this festival was John Wummer, of the New York Philharmonic. I was excited to be asked to fill in for him. Pablo Casals conducted Beethoven's Symphony no. 9, the Bach *St. Matthew Passion*, and Brahms's Symphony no. 1. Robert Shaw brought his Cleveland Orchestra Chorus for the vocal extravaganzas, and he led the Fauré *Requiem*. Another conductor was Alexander Schneider. The soloist list was also outstanding, with Maureen Forrester, Isaac Stern, Rudolph Serkin, William Warfield, etc. And what a wonderful orchestra, with Frank Miller as principal cello, Mason Jones from Philadelphia on French horn, Sidney Harth as concertmaster, and so on through the whole group.

The makeup of the flute section was uncanny. I went in as principal flute. On second chair was Lois Schaefer, who was then principal flute with the New York City Opera. She later went to the Boston Symphony on piccolo. The third flutist was Felix Skowronek. He was then teaching at the Puerto Rico Conservatory of Music, and later went to the University of Washington in Seattle. Lois had been my teacher when I was a wee lad of ten in little Yakima, Washington. Felix had studied with me in the summers, when I was home in Seattle after attending the Curtis Institute in Philadelphia. What god or demon thought up the coincidence of putting us in the same flute section?

We played several concerts in San Juan and then popped over to Santo Domingo in the Dominican Republic. A tyrannical dictator, Trujillo, ruled the country at that time. The city was under heavy restraint by both police and the military. It had a frightening ambience. We found it best to stay on the hotel grounds. The concert hall was surrounded by an iron fence and guarded by soldiers. We played, under Robert Shaw, the Fauré *Requiem*, and under Pablo Casals, the Beethoven Symphony no. 9. After the concert we returned immediately to the hotel and prayed that we could get out of Santo Domingo in the morning. A revolt with many deaths shook the country only a short time after we left.

When the scheduling ended in Puerto Rico we were shipped off to New York City, where we performed the Bach *St. Matthew Passion* at Carnegie Hall under Pablo Casals. It had been several inspiring weeks of music making.

Casals was not a great conductor but he had an aura that communicated itself to the orchestra and to the audiences. He was of the school that didn't consider the style of each composer. That was par for the course at the time of his training. Everything that he performed was by Pablo Casals. The Bach was the Beethoven was the Brahms. It all had a great romantic fervor. On the other hand, technical stylists often go too far and end up boring the audience. Perhaps something in between is to be considered.

My next big festival experience was in 1970, when I went to Carmel-by-the-Sea in California for the Carmel Bach Festival. My experiences here affected my life even more than did those in Santa Fe, as Carmel became my second home for many years because of the people there with whom I bonded. The festival was organized and conducted by a pleasant and musically satisfying Hungarian gentleman, Sandor Salgo. He lived in California and did most of his conducting in that state. Bach was the main composer at the festivals, but not exclusively so.

My first year, with Anne Adams, harpist of the San Francisco Symphony, I played the Mozart Concerto for flute and harp. I also did a flute recital and some chamber music. The orchestra performed many works, including, over my three-year period, Bach's Mass in b minor, his *St. Matthew Passion*, and his *St. John Passion*. It was high-level music making, with audiences coming from both southern and northern California to enjoy the music and the entrancing setting of Carmel, 125 miles south of San Francisco.

It was here that I met the dear lady, Katherine Lewis, who in the early '80s commissioned Morton Gould to write a flute concerto for me. The beautiful and eventually sad tale of this dear friend I have told elsewhere in this tome, in chapter 11, "Solo Dates." The artist David Ligare and the sculptor Gary Smith also became good friends, music lovers that they are. I have a four-by-five-foot painting in my living room that David did for me in the late '70s. But most fulfilling was meeting William Samuel. He took a month away from his job each summer so he could donate his services to the Carmel Bach Festival. Need I say that he was a music lover? He even claimed to like my two performances of the Mozart D Major Flute Concerto at the festival in 1971!

At that period in my career I was becoming slightly tired of Beethoven's Fifth Symphony, though I still loved music. I needed something new. With his knowledge, Bill provided that. He was a big opera nut and drew me into that fold. We took trips for opera performances, to New York, London, Paris, San Francisco, Ottawa, Santa Fe, Seattle, Chicago, etc. How grateful I am to him for opening up a whole new field of music to me. Nature, or fate, or something, can be so satisfying, letting us meet the correct new person just when he is needed.

I skipped a few years of the festival, going back in 1979 for my final summer. Besides recitals and chamber music, I did two performances of the Telemann Suite in a minor for flute and strings. I still return to the Carmel-Monterey area for visits. It is a lovely place, with great restaurants, fabulous beaches on the Pacific Ocean, and friendly people.

There was a three-week woodwind festival at the University of Wisconsin–Madison in June and July of 1973. I was offered the flute chair, got released from Ravinia, and accepted. The classes were composed of players from across the United States. They were of a very fine caliber, including young professionals who wanted to be "finished off," or boosted to a higher level. I enjoyed coaching them in flute and in chamber music. In addition, I gave a recital program during each of the three weeks.

This was rewarding as I got to work with two former friends, cellist Lowell Creitz and soprano Ilona Kombrink. Ilona and I had been students together at the Curtis Institute. She had a gorgeous, full voice. I felt that eventually she might have gone into Strauss or Wagner. She decided that she didn't want the "rat race" of the opera world and went to teach at the University of Wisconsin, where she was happily married and comfortable. We did a program together. She sounded wonderful.

Lowell I had met when we were in the U.S. Marine Band and Symphony in Washington, D.C., in the early '50s. He played a baritone in the band but his real instrument, cello, he played in the symphony. We had done many flute, cello, and piano recitals during those years in Washington, D.C., and after our program together in Madison we teamed up with the excellent pianist of that evening, Michael Keller, forming the Lydian Trio. We did many concert tours over the years.

It was a busy time at this festival with all of the flute coaching, the recital rehearsals, and the actual programs each week. In addition, I had previously committed to play the Debussy Sonata for flute, viola, and harp at the Ravinia Festival. So, the day after the second week's flute recital in Madison, I rushed back to Chicago to rehearse the Debussy, performed it a day later, and then ran back to the University of Wisconsin. A bit of a panic, but that was the life. It was exciting.

Victoria, in British Columbia, Canada, was host in the '80s to a yearly two-week event called the Victoria International Festival. Performers from Canada and the United States coached students, privately and in classes, and gave concerts. I participated in July of 1983. One week, in a recital, I did my arrangement of Debussy's *Bilitis* for flute, piano, and narrator. The following week I played the Franck Sonata in A Major with pianist Rachelle McCabe. Yondani Butt led the Festival Orchestra, with which I performed the Mozart Concerto no. 2 in D Major.

Victoria is a charming smaller city at the southern point of Vancouver Island. It is "veddy veddy" British, civilized and gracious. Around the bay are a host of flower gardens and forests with a myriad of walking paths. This atmosphere, combined with friendly and accomplished festival musicians, made for a "to be remembered" two-week period.

A similar festival occurred every summer in Jackson Hole, Wyoming, called the Grand Teton Festival. I was involved in June of 1987 for the Orchestra Seminar, which occupied the first two weeks of the festival. It was announced that "famed performers" from across the United States would be the principals of each section of the orchestra. The other chairs were filled by talented students, who would supposedly learn what was required of an orchestra player by sitting and working with the experienced first chairs.

It was indeed a wonderful group: Myron Bloom, French horn in the Cleveland Orchestra; Anthony Gigliotti, clarinet in the Philadelphia Orchestra; Leonard Sharrow, bassoon, formerly of the Pittsburgh and Chicago Symphonies; John Mack, oboe in the Cleveland Orchestra; and Donald Peck, flute in the Chicago Symphony Orchestra. We were inspired to match the standard of all of our colleagues and in doing so raised our own level. It was a fine experience for all of us, with much camaraderie and the spectacular Grand Teton Mountains as a backdrop, almost like stage scenery.

For two weeks each summer in the years 1996 and 1997, Boston University invited me to take part in the Summer Institute at the Tanglewood

Music Festival, summer home of the Boston Symphony Orchestra, in Western Massachusetts. I shared the load of giving daily master classes to flute students from all over the United States with Doriot Dwyer, long-time principal flutist of the Boston Symphony Orchestra, who had recently retired from the orchestra. I had known her for years. We got along great. She is so witty, and lots of fun to socialize with. We had many a fine dinner after a day of master classes at Tanglewood.

I was given the use of a small apartment in a huge private home in the heart of Stockbridge, about five miles from Tanglewood. Stockbridge was incorporated in 1739 and has a great many very old buildings. It simply reeked of colonialism! I walked around and through the whole area several times during the two summers, soaking up the aura of early America. This was a most enjoyable history lesson.

Whenever one of us from the Chicago Symphony played a summer festival, we could get leave from the Ravinia Festival for only a few weeks. We were doing much recording in the summer during those years, mainly with James Levine and Seiji Ozawa. The "powers" wanted to make sure that we were available for those sessions. With Jimmy we issued twenty-two CDs comprising thirty selections. With Seiji it was eleven CDs and seventeen pieces.

In 1999 Kathryn Lukas, one of the two flute teachers at Indiana University in Bloomington, took a leave of absence during the autumn semester. I was invited to fill in for her. The School of Music at Indiana University has a fine reputation. It is a large school with notable performer-teachers and a broad expanse of opportunities for the students, such as five orchestras, including Baroque and Contemporary, an outstanding opera wing, and a dedicated chamber music and recital focus. I was pleased to be a part of this for that one semester.

I had eighteen students to teach privately each week. In addition, the other flutist on the faculty, Thomas Robertello, suggested that I should give a master class each week instead of the usual every-other-week routine, since I was only on faculty for a few months. This would give each player a chance to play for me at least twice. I had busy days at Indiana.

So I devised a scheme that was a disaster! I planned to have three days a week in Chicago, doing my teaching at DePaul University, then four days in Bloomington, and so on for the twelve weeks. Chicago and Bloomington are 235 miles apart. That is four hours' driving time on a boringly straight expressway filled with roaring trucks.

I should have done two weeks in Bloomington and then one week in Chicago, etc. As it was, all of that teaching, plus the 470-mile trek, just about did me in by the end of three weeks. I then bowed to nature. I left my car in Bloomington and flew to Chicago and back each week. It wasn't much shorter in time but it was certainly easier on the mind and body, and the car too.

In 2000, and again in 2003, I spent a week at the New World Symphony in South Beach, Miami, Florida. It titles itself "America's Orchestral Academy." It is a training orchestra for young musicians hoping to make a career in an orchestra. On the first visit I coached the flutes in private sessions. Then I rehearsed with some of the strings students for two chamber music concerts. I was most impressed with their playing, plus their cooperative and musical attitude.

In 2003 I was one of six coaches, all members of major orchestras in the U.S. I handled all of the woodwind instrumentalists of the training orchestra. The first day I heard the players in a mock audition. On succeeding days I coached each one privately about the audition, about auditions in general, and about his instrument. Each was a fine player, again with that idea to learn something new. It was a rewarding experience for me. It was in October. I am only sorry that it wasn't in February!

In 2002 I spent three weeks in Australia. This was my fourth visit to that country. The first time, years ago, was on a vacation. I fell in love with the place immediately. I returned to Sydney a few years later, in 1972, to work for the Australian Radio Commission for a month. I coached the flutes and woodwinds of the Australian Training Orchestra, recorded a Mozart flute concerto with the Australian Radio Commission, and ran south to Melbourne to give two master classes. I was still in love with Australia. The third trip was on tour with the Chicago Symphony Orchestra in 1988; the full story is told in chapter 3, "Touring the World."

I was concerned about returning to Australia in 2002, as fourteen years had passed since the orchestra tour. I was worried that the environment and attitude might have altered. But no, the people were just as charming as I had remembered.

My first stop was Sydney. I walked miles every day to view any physical changes and to recapture the essence of the non-changes. I then spent a week fifty miles north of Sydney, at the University of Newcastle. I gave master classes for all instruments, coached the flutes, conducted a chamber music group, and gave a flute recital with a marvelous pianist, Colin Spiers. The staff was warm and gracious. I felt like I had known them for years. The wonderful flutist on the faculty, James Kortum, took me on a jaunt to the west, the Hunter Valley wine country.

After that week I went back "home," to Sydney. I gave a master class for the New South Wales Flute Club, saw friends, dined and wined. The time came to leave. I could have stayed on and on. Thirty years had elapsed since my first vacation trip to that country. Naturally, growth had taken place in the communities, but this didn't destroy the atmosphere in Sydney. Maybe the comparative isolation of the country, way "down under," accounts for their attention to each other. I hope to return another time. But it *is* a long journey.

Now that you are "in the know," would you say that our schedules weren't especially busy? These extra musical jobs were happening simultaneously with the orchestra schedule. We would run out of town for a class or solo date and come rushing back for the next CSO service. Our teaching hours each week were definitely adjusted to accommodate that schedule.

Another problem occurred in the university teaching routine when the orchestra toured. This could take from two to six weeks. All of those student flute lessons had to be made up. You didn't just cancel them. If I only had four pupils and we had a tour of four weeks, there would be sixteen lessons to re-schedule upon our return, besides the regular ones.

An extra job in the city had to be worked in too, if possible, since if you declined a few times you were not called again, fostering loss of income and presence. Then we had to find time to practice our instrument. And occasionally, we also wanted to live! Selfish of us, wasn't it? But I wouldn't have missed it for the world. It was certainly the right time!

In one of my schedule books I found a month that was busy but not at all uncommon. Let me lay it out for you, to give an idea of our musical lives, orchestra, teaching, and solo events. This is from February 1 to March 1, 1981.

February
1. Trio concert, Orchestra Hall, Chicago
2. DePaul University, AM flute teaching. PM master class
3. Chicago Symphony rehearsal. Evening rehearsal, Evanston Symphony,Concerto
4. CSO rehearsal. Afternoon, two-hour Civic coaching session
5. CSO rehearsal. CSO evening concert
6. CSO afternoon concert. Evanston Symphony evening concert, Concerto
7. Chamber Players rehearsal. CSO evening concert
8. Columbia, S.C., Chicago Symphony Chamber Players concert

9. CSO concert, Milwaukee, Wisconsin

10. CSO rehearsal, DePaul University teaching

11. CSO rehearsal, Civic coaching session

12. CSO rehearsal, CSO evening concert

13. CSO evening concert

14. CSO evening concert

15. Detroit, MI, Chicago Symphony Chamber Players concert

16. Toronto, Canada, Chicago Symphony Chamber Players concert

17. CSO rehearsal, Chicago, DePaul University teaching

18. Two CSO rehearsals, Civic coaching session

19. CSO rehearsal, CSO evening concert

20. CSO afternoon concert

21. Recording with Claudio Abbado, 10 to 1, and 2 to 5

22. CSO afternoon concert, DePaul University teaching

23. Recording 10 to 1, and 2 to 5

24 to 28, vacation in Seattle

March
March 1 Master class for Seattle Flute Society

13

Rondo Finale

All those rehearsals—all those concerts—so many hours of private practice, chamber music dates and solo recitals, recordings—sometimes traumas or disappointments. But there were so many glorious experiences that overshadowed the downside events, we just forgot about the negatives. We loved our careers.

In the late '50s, classical music in the United States was on a big upswing. We were a healthy, positive nation looking to the future. We had five very fine orchestras, which in the '60s developed into five great ones. They were the equal of, or superior to, any in the world: Boston, Chicago, Cleveland, New York, and Philadelphia. Continuing the trend were Cincinnati, Minneapolis, Pittsburgh, Saint Louis, San Francisco, Los Angeles, Atlanta, Detroit, Houston, and Washington, D.C. Many more followed.

The opera companies also thrived during the upswing. There were the Metropolitan Opera Company in New York, the Lyric Opera of Chicago, the San Francisco Opera, and the New York City Opera, closely followed by companies in Houston, Dallas, Seattle, San Diego, Boston, Cleveland, and Philadelphia, not to forget the wonderful Santa Fe Opera, operating for several weeks each summer. It was an exhilarating time!

Those of us in the "biz" were much involved in music making. It became a major part of our lives. So it was with trepidation that we noticed the field starting a downward trend in the early 1990s. Maybe the cliché "What goes up must come down" was applicable in this case, but we nevertheless asked, "What happened?"

Some of the smaller orchestras were affected more severely by the downturn, such as Buffalo, Denver, Kansas City, San Antonio, and San Diego. They curtailed their seasons or, in a few cases, went out of business. Some have revived, perhaps on a diminished level.

My colleagues and I discussed this issue of falling attendance on many occasions, but never seemed to latch onto an exact reason. Among those mentioned were the re-shaping of the school curriculum to eliminate music, the cacophonous essence of some contemporary programming, the big rise in ticket prices, the aging of a loyal group of audience members, the push for rock and rap, the overabundance of recordings. Who can name them all? Perhaps it was a combination of reasons. Yet the decline did happen.

Since I am away from the orchestra field now, it is only history for me. But, having been a part of the music scene of the United States, I experienced the grand gesture and climb, the highs from the late 1960s, and the gradual diminution in the 1990s.

In this writing I hope that I have presented an interesting summary of the glory of those years, the thrill of having been involved in them and maybe even contributing to them. Plus a few good stories. It makes one humble and appreciative to have been in THE RIGHT PLACE at THE RIGHT TIME!

Appendix 1. Orchestral Recordings

Chicago Symphony Orchestra
Donald Peck, Flute

Composer	Composition	Conductor	Soloist
Albéniz	*Iberia:* Navarra	Reiner	
Albéniz	*Iberia:* Fête-Dieu à Seville	Reiner	
Albéniz	*Iberia:* Triana	Reiner	
Bach	Brandenburg Concerto no. 2	Levine	
Bach	Brandenburg Concerto no. 5	Levine	
Bach	*St. Matthew Passion*	Solti	
Bach	Mass in B Minor	Solti	
Badings	Concerto for flute and wind ensemble	DeRoche	Donald Peck
Barber	*The Lovers*	Schenck	
Barber	*Prayers of Kierkegaard*	Schenck	
Bartók	*The Miraculous Mandarin*	Martinon	
Bartók	*The Miraculous Mandarin*	Boulez	
Bartók	Concerto for orchestra	Ozawa	
Bartók	Concerto for orchestra	Levine	
Bartók	Concerto for orchestra	Boulez	
Bartók	Concerto for orchestra	Solti	
Bartók	Violin Concerto no. 1	Solti	Kyung Wha Chung
Bartók	Piano Concerto no. 1	Ozawa	P. Serkin
Bartók	Piano Concerto no. 1	Abbado	Pollini
Bartók	Piano Concerto no. 2	Abbado	Pollini
Bartók	Piano Concerto no. 3	Ozawa	P. Serkin
Bartók	*Bluebeard's Castle*	Boulez	J. Norman
Bartók	*The Wooden Prince*	Boulez	
Bartók	*Hungarian Sketches*	Reiner	
Bartók	*Hungarian Sketches*	Solti	
Bartók	Four Orchestral Pieces	Boulez	
Bartók	*Dance* suite	Solti	
Bartók	*Rumanian Folk Dances*	Solti	
Beethoven	Symphony no. 1	Reiner (1961)	

Composer	Composition	Conductor	Soloist
Beethoven	Symphony no. 1	Solti (1974)	
Beethoven	Symphony no. 1	Solti (1989)	
Beethoven	Symphony no. 2	Solti (1974)	
Beethoven	Symphony no. 2	Solti (1990)	
Beethoven	Symphony no. 3	Solti (1974)	
Beethoven	Symphony no. 3	Solti (1989)	
Beethoven	Symphony no. 4	Solti (1974)	
Beethoven	Symphony no. 4	Solti (1987)	
Beethoven	Symphony no. 5	Reiner	
Beethoven	Symphony no. 5	Ozawa	
Beethoven	Symphony no. 5	Solti (1973)	
Beethoven	Symphony no. 5	Solti (1986)	
Beethoven	Symphony no. 6	Reiner	
Beethoven	Symphony no. 6	Solti (1974)	
Beethoven	Symphony no. 6	Solti (1988)	
Beethoven	Symphony no. 7	Giulini	
Beethoven	Symphony no. 7	Solti (1974)	
Beethoven	Symphony no. 7	Solti (1988)	
Beethoven	Symphony no. 8	Solti (1973)	
Beethoven	Symphony no. 8	Solti (1988)	
Beethoven	Symphony no. 9	Reiner	
Beethoven	Symphony no. 9	Solti (1972)	
Beethoven	Symphony no. 9	Solti (1986)	
Beethoven	*Coriolan Overture*	Reiner	
Beethoven	*Coriolan Overture*	Solti	
Beethoven	*Egmont Overture*	Solti (1972)	
Beethoven	*Egmont Overture*	Solti (1989)	
Beethoven	*Leonore Overture* no. 3	Solti (1972)	
Beethoven	*Leonore Overture* no. 3	Solti (1988)	
Beethoven	*Missa solemnis*	Barenboim	
Beethoven	*Missa solemnis*	Solti	
Beethoven	*Fidelio*, complete	Solti	
Beethoven	Violin Concerto	Barenboim	Zukerman
Beethoven	complete piano concerti	Solti	Ashkenazy
Beethoven	complete piano concerti	Levine	Brendel
Beethoven	Piano Concerto no. 3	Hendl	Graffman
Beethoven	Piano Concerto no. 4	Reiner	Cliburn
Beethoven	Piano Concerto no. 5	Reiner	Cliburn
Berg	Violin Concerto	Solti	Kyung Wha Chung

Composer	Composition	Conductor	Soloist
Berg	Violin Concerto	Levine	Mutter
Berio	*Continuo*	Barenboim	
Berlioz	*La damnation de Faust*	Solti	
Berlioz	*Les nuits d'été*	Reiner	L. Price
Berlioz	*Symphonie fantastique*	Solti (1972)	
Berlioz	*Symphonie fantastique*	Solti (1992)	
Berlioz	*Symphonie fantastique*	Barenboim	
Berlioz	*Symphonie fantastique*	Abbado	
Berlioz	*Romeo and Juliet*, orchestral music	Giulini	
Bizet	*L'Arlesienne*, suites 1 and 2	Martinon	
Bizet	Symphony in C Major	Martinon	
Borodin	*Polovtsian Dances*	Barenboim	
Borodin	*Polovtsian Dances*	Ozawa	
Borodin	*Prince Igor*, act 3, Polovski March	Reiner	
Brahms	Piano Concerto no. 1	Leinsdorf	Berman
Brahms	Piano Concerto no. 1	Levine	Ax
Brahms	Piano Concerto no. 2	Reiner	Cliburn
Brahms	Piano Concerto no. 2	Leinsdorf	Richter
Brahms	Piano Concerto no. 2	Reiner	Gilels
Brahms	Violin Concerto	Giulini	Perlman
Brahms	Violin Concerto	Barenboim	Vengerov
Brahms	Double Concerto	Barenboim	Perlman, Ma
Brahms	*Hungarian Dances*	Barenboim	
Brahms	*German Requiem*	Solti	
Brahms	*German Requiem*	Levine	
Brahms	*German Requiem*	Barenboim	
Brahms	Symphony no. 1	Solti	
Brahms	Symphony no. 1	Barenboim	
Brahms	Symphony no. 1	Wand	
Brahms	Symphony no. 1	Levine	
Brahms	Symphony no. 2	Solti	
Brahms	Symphony no. 2	Barenboim	
Brahms	Symphony no. 2	Levine	
Brahms	Symphony no. 3	Solti	
Brahms	Symphony no. 3	Barenboim	
Brahms	Symphony no. 3	Levine	
Brahms	Symphony no. 4	Solti	
Brahms	Symphony no. 4	Barenboim	

Composer	Composition	Conductor	Soloist
Brahms	Symphony no. 4	Giulini	
Brahms	Symphony no. 4	Levine	
Brahms	*Tragic Overture*	Barenboim	
Brahms	*Tragic Overture*	Solti	
Brahms	*Academic Festival Overture*	Barenboim	
Brahms	*Academic Festival Overture*	Solti	
Brahms	Variations on a Theme of Haydn	Solti	
Brahms	Variations on a Theme of Haydn	Barenboim	
Brahms/ Schoenberg	Piano Quartet in G Minor	Craft	
Britten	*A Young Person's Guide to the Orchestra*	Ozawa	
Bruch	*Kol nidrei*	Levine	Haimovitz
Bruch	Violin Concerto no. 1	Slatkin	Lin
Bruch	Violin Concerto no. 1	Abbado	Mintz
Bruch	*Scottish Fantasy*	Slatkin	Lin
Bruckner	*Te deum*	Barenboim	
Bruckner	Symphony no. 0	Solti	
Bruckner	Symphony no. 0	Barenboim	
Bruckner	Symphony no. 1	Solti	
Bruckner	Symphony no. 1	Barenboim	
Bruckner	Symphony no. 2	Solti	
Bruckner	Symphony no. 2	Barenboim	
Bruckner	Symphony no. 3	Solti	
Bruckner	Symphony no. 3	Barenboim	
Bruckner	Symphony no. 4	Solti	
Bruckner	Symphony no. 4	Barenboim	
Bruckner	Symphony no. 5	Solti	
Bruckner	Symphony no. 5	Barenboim	
Bruckner	Symphony no. 6	Solti	
Bruckner	Symphony no. 6	Barenboim	
Bruckner	Symphony no. 7	Solti	
Bruckner	Symphony no. 7	Barenboim	
Bruckner	Symphony no. 8	Solti	
Bruckner	Symphony no. 8	Barenboim	
Bruckner	Symphony no. 9	Giulini	
Bruckner	Symphony no. 9	Solti	
Bruckner	Symphony no. 9	Barenboim	

Composer	Composition	Conductor	Soloist
Carter	*Partita*	Barenboim	
Chausson	Poem for violin and orchestra	Barenboim	Perlman
Chopin	Piano Concerto no. 2	Abbado	Pogorelich
Copland	*Dance* Symphony	Gould	
Corigliano	Symphony no. 1	Barenboim	
Debussy	*La mer*	Reiner	
Debussy	*La mer*	Solti (1976)	
Debussy	*La mer*	Solti (1990)	
Debussy	*Nocturnes*	Solti	
Debussy	Symphonies nos. 1, 2, and 3 (Chamber Symphony of Chicago)	Faldner	
Debussy	*Prelude to the Afternoon of a Faun*	Solti (1976)	
Debussy	*Prelude to the Afternoon of a Faun*	Solti (1990)	
Del Tredici	*Final Alice*	Solti	
Dohnányi	Variations on a Nursery Song	Solti	Schiff
Dvořák	Cello Concerto	Barenboim	Du Pré
Dvořák	*Silent Woods*	Barenboim	Du Pré
Dvořák	*Slavonic Dances*	Barenboim	
Dvořák	Symphony no. 7	Levine	
Dvořák	Symphony no. 8	Giulini	
Dvořák	Symphony no. 9	Levine	
Dvořák	Symphony no. 9	Giulini	
Dvořák	Symphony no. 9	Solti	
Elgar	*Enigma Variations*	Solti	
Elgar	Violin Concerto	Barenboim	Perlman
Falla	*El amor brujo*	Reiner	L. Price
Falla	*Nights in the Gardens of Spain*	Domingo	Barenboim
Falla	*The Three-Cornered Hat*, complete	Barenboim	Larmore
Falla	*The Three-Cornered Hat*, dances only	Reiner	
Franck	Symphony in D Minor	Monteux	
Glinka	*Russlan und Ludmilla*, overture	Reiner	
Gould	*Spirituals for Orchestra*	Gould	

Composer	Composition	Conductor	Soloist
Gounod	*Petite symphonie* (Chamber Symphony of Chicago)	Faldner	
Granados	*Goyescas*, intermezzo	Reiner	
Haydn	*The Creation*	Solti (1981)	
Haydn	*The Creation*	Solti (1993)	
Haydn	*The Seasons*	Solti	
Haydn	Symphony no. 88	Reiner	
Hindemith	*Nobilissima visione*	Martinon	
Holst	*The Planets*	Levine	
Hovhaness	*Mysterious Mountain*	Reiner	
Ives	Orchestral Set no. 2	Gould	
Ives	*Robert Browning Overture*	Gould	
Ives	*Putnam's Camp*	Gould	
Ives	Symphony no. 1	Gould	
Ives	Symphony no. 1	Tilson Thomas	
Ives	*Holiday* symphony	Tilson Thomas	
Ives	*The Unanswered Question*	Tilson Thomas	
Ives	*The Unanswered Question*	Gould	
Ives	Symphony no. 4	Tilson Thomas	
Ives	*Central Park in the Dark*	Tilson Thomas	
Ives	Variations on "America"	Gould	
Janáček	*Sinfonietta*	Ozawa	
Kabalevsky	*Colas Breugnon Overture*	Reiner	
Kodály	*Dances of Galánta*	Ozawa	
Kodály	*Dances of Galánta*	Järvi	
Kodály	*Peacock Variations*	Järvi	
Kodály	*Háry János* suite	Järvi	
Kodály	*Háry János* suite	Solti	
Lalo	*Le roi d'Ys*, overture	Martinon	
Lalo	*Symphonie espagnole*	Hendl	Szeryng
Liszt	*Mephisto Waltz*	Solti	
Liszt	Hungarian Rhapsody no. 2	Solti	
Liszt	*Faust* symphony	Solti	
Liszt	*Les preludes*	Solti	
Liszt	*Les preludes*	Barenboim	
Liszt	*Totentanz*	Reiner	Janis
Lutoslawski	Symphony no. 3	Barenboim	
Lutoslawski	Concerto for orchestra	Ozawa	
Lutoslawski	Concerto for orchestra	Barenboim	
MacDowell	Piano Concerto no. 2	Hendl	Cliburn

Composer	Composition	Conductor	Soloist
Mahler	Symphony no. 1	Solti	
Mahler	Symphony no. 1	Giulini	
Mahler	Symphony no. 1	Abbado	
Mahler	Symphony no. 1	Boulez	
Mahler	Symphony no. 1	Tennstedt	
Mahler	Symphony no. 2	Solti	
Mahler	Symphony no. 2	Abbado	
Mahler	Symphony no. 3	Levine	
Mahler	Symphony no. 3	Solti	
Mahler	Symphony no. 4	Reiner	
Mahler	Symphony no. 4	Levine	
Mahler	Symphony no. 4	Solti	
Mahler	Symphony no. 5	Solti (1970)	
Mahler	Symphony no. 5	Solti (1990)	
Mahler	Symphony no. 5	Abbado	
Mahler	Symphony no. 5	Barenboim	
Mahler	Symphony no. 6	Solti	
Mahler	Symphony no. 6	Abbado	
Mahler	Symphony no. 7	Solti	
Mahler	Symphony no. 7	Abbado	
Mahler	Symphony no. 7	Levine	
Mahler	Symphony no. 8	Solti	
Mahler	Symphony no. 9	Boulez	
Mahler	Symphony no. 9	Solti	
Mahler	Symphony no. 9	Giulini	
Mahler	Symphony no. 10	Martinon	
Mahler	*Des Knaben Wunderhorn,* our songs	Solti	Minton
Mahler	*Rückert Lieder*	Abbado	Schwartz
Mahler	*Songs of a Wayfarer*	Solti	Minton
Mahler	*Das Lied von der Erde*	Reiner	Forrester, Lewis
Mahler	*Das Lied von der Erde*	Barenboim	Meier, Jerusalem
Mahler	*Das Lied von der Erde*	Solti	Minton, Kollo
Mahler	*Totenfeier*	Boulez	
Martin	Concerto for seven winds	Martinon	
Martinon	Symphony no. 4	Martinon	
Massenet	*Thaïs,* Meditation	Martinon	

Composer	Composition	Conductor	Soloist
Mendelssohn	*A Midsummer Night's Dream*, incidental music	Martinon	
Mendelssohn	*A Midsummer Night's Dream*, overture	Barenboim	
Mendelssohn	*A Midsummer Night's Dream*, complete	Levine	
Mendelssohn	Violin Concerto	Abbado	Mintz
Mendelssohn	Violin Concerto	Barenboim	Perlman
Mendelssohn	Symphony no. 3	Solti	
Mendelssohn	Symphony no. 4	Solti	
Mennin	Symphony no. 7	Martinon	
Miaskovsky	Symphony no. 21	Gould	
Milhaud	Symphony no. 1 (Chamber Symphony of Chicago)	Faldner	
Milhaud	Symphony no. 2 (Chamber Symphony of Chicago)	Faldner	
Milhaud	Symphony no. 3 (Chamber Symphony of Chicago)	Faldner	
Mozart	Symphony no. 38	Solti	
Mozart	Symphony no. 39	Solti	
Mozart	Symphony no. 40	Levine	
Mozart	Symphony no. 41	Levine	
Mozart	Piano Concerto no. 25, K. 503	Reiner	Tchaikowsky
Mozart	*Don Giovanni*, overture	Reiner	
Mozart	*The Marriage of Figaro*, overture	Reiner	
Mussorgsky	*Pictures at an Exhibition*	Reiner	
Mussorgsky	*Pictures at an Exhibition*	Solti	
Mussorgsky	*Pictures at an Exhibition*	Ozawa	
Mussorgsky	*Pictures at an Exhibition*	Giulini	
Mussorgsky	*Pictures at an Exhibition*	Järvi	
Mussorgsky	*A Night on Bare Mountain*	Reiner	
Mussorgsky	*A Night on Bare Mountain*	Barenboim	
Mussorgsky	*A Night on Bare Mountain*	Ozawa	
Mussorgsky	*Khovanschina*, prelude	Solti	
Nicolai	*The Merry Wives of Windsor*, overture	Barenboim	
Nielsen	Symphony no. 2	Gould	

Composer	Composition	Conductor	Soloist
Nielsen	Symphony no. 4	Martinon	
Nielsen	Clarinet Concerto	Gould	Goodman
Nielsen	*Helios Overture*	Martinon	
Paganini	Violin Concerto no. 1	Hendl	Friedman
Prokofiev	*Alexander Nevsky*	Reiner	
Prokofiev	*Scythian* suite	Abbado	
Prokofiev	*Lieutenant Kije* suite	Abbado	
Prokofiev	*Romeo and Juliet* suite	Solti	
Prokofiev	Symphony no. 1 (classical)	Solti	
Prokofiev	Symphony no. 1 (classical)	Giulini	
Prokofiev	Symphony no. 1 (classical)	Levine	
Prokofiev	Symphony no. 5	Levine	
Prokofiev	Piano Concerto no. 3	Hendl	Cliburn
Prokofiev	Violin Concerto no. 1	Abbado	Mintz
Prokofiev	Violin Concerto no. 2	Abbado	Mintz
Prokofiev	Violin Concerto no. 2	Barenboim	Perlman
Rachmaninoff	Piano Concerto no. 2	Reiner	Cliburn
Rachmaninoff	Piano Concerto no. 2	Abbado	Licad
Rachmaninoff	Piano Concerto no. 3	Pretre	Weissenberg
Rachmaninoff	Rhapsody on a Theme of Paganini	Abbado	Licad
Ravel	*Daphnis and Chloe,* suite no. 2	Martinon	
Ravel	*Daphnis and Chloe,* suite no. 2 (CSO CD)	Solti	
Ravel	*Daphnis and Chloe,* suite no. 2	Barenboim	
Ravel	*Alborada del gracioso*	Martinon	
Ravel	*Alborada del gracioso*	Barenboim	
Ravel	*Le tombeau de couperin*	Solti	
Ravel	*Mother Goose,* suite	Martinon	
Ravel	*Bolero*	Barenboim	
Ravel	*Bolero*	Solti	
Ravel	*Rhapsodie espagnole*	Martinon	
Ravel	*Rhapsodie espagnole*	Barenboim	
Ravel	*Pavane for a Dead Princess*	Barenboim	
Ravel	*Pavane for a Dead Princess*	Martinon	
Ravel	*La valse*	Martinon	
Ravel	Introduction and Allegro	Martinon	Druzinsky
Respighi	*The Pines of Rome*	Reiner	

Composer	Composition	Conductor	Soloist
Respighi	*The Fountains of Rome*	Reiner	
Rihm	Concerto for violin	Levine	Mutter
Rimsky-Korsakov	*Scheherazade*	Reiner	
Rimsky-Korsakov	*Scheherazade*	Barenboim	
Rimsky-Korsakov	*Scheherazade*	Ozawa	
Rimsky-Korsakov	*Russian Easter Overture*	Stokowski	
Rimsky-Korsakov	*Russian Easter Overture*	Barenboim	
Rimsky-Korsakov	*Capriccio espagnol*	Barenboim	
Rimsky-Korsakov	Symphony no. 2 (*Antar*)	Gould	
Rimsky-Korsakov	*Tsar Sultan*, suite	Barenboim	
Rossini	*William Tell Overture*	Reiner	
Rossini	*Silken Ladder Overture*	Reiner	
Rossini	*Il Signor Bruschino*, overture	Reiner	
Rossini	*The Barber of Seville*, overture	Reiner	
Rossini	*The Barber of Seville*, overture	Solti	
Rossini	*La gazza ladra*, overture	Reiner	
Rossini	*La Cenerentola*, overture	Reiner	
Roussel	*Bacchus et Ariane*, suite no. 2	Martinon	
Saint-Saëns	Symphony no. 3 (*Organ*)	Barenboim	
Saint-Saëns	Introduction and Rondo capriccioso	Hendl	Friedman
Saint-Saëns	Cello Concerto	Levine	Haimovitz
Schmidt	Symphony no. 2	Järvi	
Schmidt	Symphony no. 3	Järvi	
Schoenberg	*Moses und Aron*	Solti	
Schoenberg	Concerto for piano	Ozawa	P. Serkin
Schoenberg	*Pelleas und Melisande*	Boulez	
Schoenberg	Five Pieces for Orchestra	Barenboim	
Schoenberg	Variations for Orchestra, Op. 31	Boulez	
Schoenberg	Variations for Orchestra, Op. 31	Solti	
Schubert	Symphony no. 4	Giulini	
Schubert	Symphony no. 5	Reiner	

Composer	Composition	Conductor	Soloist
Schubert	Symphony no. 8	Reiner	
Schubert	Symphony no. 8	Ozawa	
Schubert	Symphony no. 8	Giulini	
Schubert	Symphony no. 9 (*The Great*)	Giulini	
Schubert	Symphony no. 9 (*The Great*)	Levine	
Schubert	*Rosamunde*, overture	Barenboim	
Schubert	*Rosamunde*, overture and ballet music	Levine	
Schumann	Symphony no. 1	Barenboim	
Schumann	Symphony no. 2	Barenboim	
Schumann	Symphony no. 3	Barenboim	
Schumann	Symphony no. 4	Barenboim	
Schumann	Piano Concerto	Reiner (1959)	Janis
Schumann	Piano Concerto	Reiner (1960)	Cliburn
Schumann	Piano Concerto	Giulini	Rubenstein
Schumann	*Manfred Overture*	Barenboim	
Scriabin	*Poem of Ecstasy*	Boulez	
Scriabin	*Poem of Ecstasy*	Järvi	
Scriabin	*Prometheus*	Boulez	
Shostakovich	Symphony no. 1	Bernstein	
Shostakovich	Symphony no. 4	Previn	
Shostakovich	Symphony no. 5	Previn	
Shostakovich	Symphony no. 6	Stokowski	
Shostakovich	Symphony no. 7	Bernstein	
Shostakovich	Symphony no. 8	Solti	
Shostakovich	Symphony no. 10	Solti	
Shostakovich	Symphony no. 10 (CSO CD)	Stokowski	
Shostakovich	Symphony no. 13	Solti	
Shostakovich	Symphony no. 15	Solti	
Shostakovich	*Songs of Dances of Death*	Solti	Aleksashkin
Sibelius	Violin Concerto	Hendl	Heifetz
Smetana	*The Moldau*	Barenboim	
Strauss, Johann	Six Waltzes	Reiner	
Strauss, Johann	Ten Waltzes	Barenboim	
Strauss, Richard	*Also sprach Zarathustra*	Reiner	
Strauss, Richard	*Also sprach Zarathustra*	Solti	

Composer	Composition	Conductor	Soloist
Strauss, Richard	*Also sprach Zarathustra*	Boulez	
Strauss, Richard	*Alpine* symphony	Barenboim	
Strauss, Richard	*Don Juan*	Reiner	
Strauss, Richard	*Don Juan*	Solti	
Strauss, Richard	*Don Juan*	Barenboim	
Strauss, Richard	*Die Frau ohne Schatten,* excerpts	Barenboim	
Strauss, Richard	*Ein Heldenleben*	Barenboim	
Strauss, Richard	*Don Quixote*	Barenboim	
Strauss, Richard	*Don Quixote*	Reiner	
Strauss, Richard	*Till Eulenspiegel's Merry Pranks*	Barenboim	
Strauss, Richard	*Till Eulenspiegel's Merry Pranks*	Solti	
Stravinsky	*The Rite of Spring*	Ozawa	
Stravinsky	*The Rite of Spring*	Solti	
Stravinsky	*Oedipus Rex,* complete	Levine	
Stravinsky	*Le baiser de la fée,* divertimento	Reiner	
Stravinsky	Four Etudes	Boulez	
Stravinsky	*The Firebird,* suite	Giulini	
Stravinsky	*The Firebird,* complete	Boulez	
Stravinsky	*Petrouchka,* complete	Levine	
Stravinsky	*Petrouchka,* complete	Solti	
Stravinsky	*Petrouchka,* suite	Giulini	
Stravinsky	*Jeu de cartes*	Solti	
Stravinsky	*Fireworks*	Ozawa	
Stravinsky	*Fireworks*	Boulez	
Stravinsky	*Orpheus*	Stravinsky	
Stravinsky	Symphony in Three Movements	Solti	
Stravinsky	Violin Concerto	Barenboim	Perlman
Takemitsu	*Visions*	Barenboim	
Tchaikovsky	*The Tempest*	Abbado	

Composer	Composition	Conductor	Soloist
Tchaikovsky	*Marche slave*	Reiner	
Tchaikovsky	*Marche slave*	Barenboim	
Tchaikovsky	*Marche slave*	Abbado	
Tchaikovsky	*Capriccio italien*	Barenboim	
Tchaikovsky	Five Waltzes	Gould	
Tchaikovsky	*1812 Overture*	Abbado	
Tchaikovsky	*1812 Overture*	Barenboim	
Tchaikovsky	*1812 Overture*	Solti	
Tchaikovsky	*Romeo and Juliet Overture—* Fantasy	Barenboim (1997)	
Tchaikovsky	*Romeo and Juliet Overture—* Fantasy	Barenboim (1981)	
Tchaikovsky	*Romeo and Juliet Overture—* Fantasy	Abbado	
Tchaikovsky	*Romeo and Juliet Overture—* Fantasy	Solti	
Tchaikovsky	*Swan Lake*, suite	Solti	
Tchaikovsky	*Voyevode*	Abbado	
Tchaikovsky	*Francesca da Rimini*	Barenboim	
Tchaikovsky	*Nutcracker*, suite	Solti	
Tchaikovsky	*Nutcracker*, suite	Abbado	
Tchaikovsky	*Nutcracker*, suite	Reiner	
Tchaikovsky	*Marche miniature*	Reiner	
Tchaikovsky	Symphony no. 1	Abbado	
Tchaikovsky	Symphony no. 2	Abbado	
Tchaikovsky	Symphony no. 3	Abbado	
Tchaikovsky	Symphony no. 4	Solti	
Tchaikovsky	Symphony no. 4	Abbado	
Tchaikovsky	Symphony no. 5	Solti (1975)	
Tchaikovsky	Symphony no. 5	Solti (1987)	
Tchaikovsky	Symphony no. 5	Ozawa	
Tchaikovsky	Symphony no. 5	Abbado	
Tchaikovsky	Symphony no. 5	Barenboim	
Tchaikovsky	Symphony no. 6	Levine	
Tchaikovsky	Symphony no. 6	Abbado	
Tchaikovsky	Symphony no. 6	Barenboim	
Tchaikovsky	Symphony no. 6	Solti	
Tchaikovsky	Piano Concerto no. 1	Solti	Schiff
Tippett	Symphony no. 4	Solti	
Tippett	*Birthday of Prince Charles*	Solti	

Composer	Composition	Conductor	Soloist
Varese	*Arcana*	Boulez	
Varese	*Arcana*	Martinon	
Varese	*Ameriques*	Boulez	
various	*Fantasia* soundtrack: Elgar, Beethoven no. 5, Saint-Saëns	Levine	
Verdi	Four Sacred Pieces	Solti	
Verdi	*Requiem*	Solti	L. Price, Luchetti, Baker, Van Dam
Verdi	*Requiem*	Barenboim	Marc, Meier, Domingo
Verdi	opera choruses	Solti	
Verdi	*Otello*	Solti	Pavarotti, Te Kanawa
Wagner	*Der fliegende Holländer,* complete	Solti	Bailey, Martin, Kollo, Tavela
Wagner	*Der fliegende Holländer,* overture	Solti	
Wagner	*Der fliegende Holländer,* overture	Barenboim	
Wagner	*Die Meistersinger von Nürnberg,* complete	Solti	VanDam, Pape, Heppner, Mattilla
Wagner	*Die Meistersinger,* overture	Solti (1972)	
Wagner	*Die Meistersinger,* overture	Solti (1977)	
Wagner	*Die Meistersinger,* overture	Barenboim	
Wagner	*Die Meistersinger,* overture	Reiner	
Wagner	*Die Meistersinger,* prelude to act 3	Reiner	
Wagner	*Die Meistersinger,* prelude to act 3	Barenboim	
Wagner	*Die Meistersinger,* Prize Song (for horn)	Barenboim	
Wagner	*Die Meistersinger,* Dance of the Apprentices	Reiner	
Wagner	*Die Meistersinger,* Procession of the Meistersingers	Reiner	
Wagner	*Die Walküre,* Ride of the Valkyries	Barenboim	

Composer	Composition	Conductor	Soloist
Wagner	*Die Götterdämmerung*, Brunnhilde's Immolation Scene	Barenboim	D. Polaski
Wagner	*Lohengrin*, prelude to act 1	Barenboim	
Wagner	*Lohengrin*, prelude to act 3	Barenboim	
Wagner	*Parsifal*, prelude	Barenboim	
Wagner	*Parsifal*, Good Friday music	Barenboim	
Wagner	*Rienzi*, overture	Barenboim	
Wagner	*Siegfried*, Forest Murmurs	Barenboim	
Wagner	*Siegfried*, Rhine Journey	Reiner	
Wagner	*Siegfried*, Rhine Journey	Barenboim	
Wagner	*Siegfried*, Siegfried's Death and Funeral Music	Reiner	
Wagner	*Siegfried*, Siegfried's Death and Funeral Music	Barenboim	
Wagner	*Siegfried* idyll	Barenboim	
Wagner	*Tannhäuser*, overture	Barenboim	
Wagner	*Tannhäuser*, overture	Solti	
Wagner	*Tannhäuser*, prelude to act 3	Barenboim	
Wagner	*Tristan und Isolde*, prelude and Liebestod	Solti	
Wagner	*Tristan und Isolde*, prelude and Liebestod	Barenboim	
Weber	Rondo Brilliant for cello and orchestra	Barenboim	Miller
Weber	*Oberon*, overture	Barenboim	
Weber	Clarinet Concerto no. 1	Martinon	Goodman
Weber	Clarinet Concerto no. 2	Martinon	Goodman

Appendix 2. Opera Performances by the Chicago Symphony Orchestra, 1957–1999

(subscription concerts at Orchestra Hall unless otherwise noted)

Claudio Abbado

BERG *Wozzeck*
   May 24, 25, and 27, 1984
MUSSORGSKY *Boris Godunov*
   November 1, 2, and 4, 1984
SCHOENBERG *Erwartung*
   February 3, 4, and 5, 1983
STRAVINSKY *Oedipus Rex*
   March 5, 6, and 7, 1981

Franz Allers

LEHÁR *The Merry Widow*
   June 7 and 9, 1967 (June Festival)
J. STRAUSS *Die Fledermaus*
   June 7 and 8, 1966 (June Festival)

Daniel Barenboim

BEETHOVEN *Fidelio*
   May 26, 28, and 31, 1998
MOZART *Così fan tutte*
   February 5 and 15, 1992
   February 10, 1992 (special)
MOZART *Don Giovanni*
   February 4 and 13, 1992
   February 8, 1992 (special)
MOZART *The Marriage of Figaro*
   February 2 and 12, 1992
   February 7, 1992 (special)
R. STRAUSS *Elektra*
   March 15, 18, and 21, 1995
   November 9, 1995 (Carnegie Hall)
WAGNER *Parsifal* (act 2)
   March 1, 2, 3, and 6, 1990

WAGNER *Tristan und Isolde* (act 2)
  November 6, 1985 (special)
  November 8, 1985
  January 14, 16, and 19, 1993

Pierre Boulez
BARTÓK *Bluebeard's Castle*
  December 2, 4, and 7, 1993
  (recorded by DG at Orchestra Hall, December 6 and 13, 1993)
SCHOENBERG *Moses und Aron*
  March 24 and 26, 1999
  April 1, 1999 (Berlin Philharmonie)

Christoph von Dohnányi
SCHOENBERG *Erwartung*
  April 12, 13, and 14, 1979

Christoph Eschenbach
BEETHOVEN *Fidelio*
  August 13, 1993 (Ravinia)
SAINT-SAËNS *Samson and Dalila* (act 2)
  August 8, 1997 (Ravinia)

Irwin Hoffman
SCHOENBERG *Erwartung*
  September 21, 1968 (special)

Antonio Janigro
PURCELL *Dido and Aeneas*
  June 15 and 17, 1967 (June Festival)

Kenneth Jean
BARTÓK *Bluebeard's Castle*
  January 28, 1989

István Kertész
BARTÓK *Bluebeard's Castle*
  July 20, 1969 (Ravinia)
VERDI *Otello*
  July 9 and 11, 1970 (Ravinia)
VERDI *Rigoletto*
  July 15 and 17, 1971 (Ravinia)

Steven Larsen
KNUSSEN *Where the Wild Things Are*
  December 22, 1988 (Auditorium Theatre)

James Levine

BELLINI *Norma*
    July 11 and 14, 1973 (Ravinia)

BERLIOZ *Les Troyens* (part 1)
    June 30, 1978 (Ravinia)

BERLIOZ *Les Troyens* (part 2)
    July 1, 1978 (Ravinia)

DONIZETTI *L'elisir d'amore*
    June 21, 1991 (Ravinia)

MOZART *The Abduction from the Seraglio*
    July 17 and 19, 1975 (Ravinia)

MOZART *Così fan tutte*
    July 16 and 18, 1975 (Ravinia)
    June 28, 1987 (Ravinia)

MOZART *Don Giovanni*
    July 8, 1988 (Ravinia)

PUCCINI *Tosca*
    July 1, 1972 (Ravinia)

SAINT-SAËNS *Samson and Dalila*
    June 27, 1992 (Ravinia)

R. STRAUSS *Ariadne auf Naxos*
    July 3, 1987 (Ravinia)

R. STRAUSS *Elektra*
    June 27, 1986 (Ravinia)

STRAVINSKY *Oedipus Rex*
    July 7, 1991 (Ravinia)
    (recorded by DG at Medinah Temple, July 8 and 9, 1991)

TCHAIKOVSKY *Eugene Onegin*
    June 27, 1980 (Ravinia)

VERDI *La forza del destino*
    June 22, 1979 (Ravinia)

VERDI *La traviata*
    July 10 and 13, 1974 (Ravinia)

VERDI *Macbeth*
    June 26, 1981 (Ravinia)

WAGNER *Die Walküre* (act 2)
    August 8, 1972 (Ravinia)
    July 1, 1988 (Ravinia)

Henry Lewis

OFFENBACH *La Périchole*
    June 1 and 3, 1966 (June Festival)

ROSSINI *L'italiana in Algeri*
June 2, 1967 (June Festival)

Alain Lombard
PUCCINI *Madama Butterfly*
July 31 and August 2, 1969 (Ravinia)

Jean Martinon
BARTÓK *Bluebeard's Castle*
April 27, 28, and 29, 1967

Henry Mazer
DONIZETTI *Don Pasquale*
May 19, 1980 (special)

Zubin Mehta
PUCCINI *Tosca*
June 24, 1995 (Ravinia)

Michael Morgan
DAVIS *X: The Life and Times of Malcolm X*
November 14 and 15, 1992 (special)
KNUSSEN *Where the Wild Things Are*
December 17, 18, 21, and 23, 1988 (Auditorium Theatre)

Giuseppe Patane
DONIZETTI *Lucia di Lammermoor*
August 6 and 8, 1970 (Ravinia)
VERDI *Aida*
August 7 and 9, 1969 (Ravinia)

Fritz Reiner
STRAVINSKY *Mavra*
October 22, 23, and 27, 1959

Sir Georg Solti
BARTÓK *Bluebeard's Castle*
April 25 and 27, 1974
May 1, 1974 (Carnegie Hall)
January 26, 27, and 30, 1989
BEETHOVEN *Fidelio*
March 12, 14, and 16, 1970
May 10 and 12, 1979 (special)
May 19, 1979 (Carnegie)
(recorded by Decca at Medinah Temple, May 21, 22, 23, and 24, 1979)
SCHOENBERG *Erwartung*
April 12 and 13, 1973

SCHOENBERG *Moses und Aron*
  November 11, 12, and 13, 1971
  November 20, 1971 (Carnegie Hall)
  April 19 and 21, 1984
  (recorded by Decca at Orchestra Hall, April 23, 24, and 30, and May 1, 1984)
R. STRAUSS *Salome*
  December 13 and 15, 1974 (special)
  December 18, 1974 (Carnegie Hall)
STRAVINSKY *Oedipus Rex*
  January 29, 30, and 31, 1976
VERDI *Falstaff*
  April 25, 26, and 27, 1985
  April 29, 1985 (Carnegie Hall)
VERDI *Otello*
  April 8 and 12, 1991 (special)
  April 16 and 19, 1991 (Carnegie Hall)
  (recorded live in concert by Decca at Orchestra Hall and Carnegie Hall, April 8, 12, 16, and 19, 1991)
WAGNER *The Flying Dutchman*
  May 6 and 8, 1976 (special)
  May 14, 1976 (Carnegie Hall)
  (recorded by Decca at Medinah Temple, May 18, 19, 21, and 22, 1976)
WAGNER *Die Götterdämmerung* (act 3)
  April 26 and 28, 1973
  May 2, 1973 (Carnegie Hall)
WAGNER *Die Meistersinger von Nürnberg* (acts 1 and 2)
  September 20, 1995 (open rehearsal)
  September 23 and 26, 1995 (special)
  (recorded live in concert by Decca at Orchestra Hall on September 20, 23, and 26, 1995)
WAGNER *Die Meistersinger von Nürnberg* (act 3)
  September 21, 1995 (open rehearsal)
  September 24 and 27, 1995 (special)
  (recorded live in concert by Decca at Orchestra Hall on September 21, 24, and 27, 1995)
WAGNER *Das Rheingold*
  April 22, 24, and 26, 1971
  April 27, 1971 (Carnegie Hall)
  April 7 and 9, 1983
  April 12, 1983 (special)
  April 18, 1983 (Carnegie Hall)
WAGNER *Siegfried* (act 3)
  April 16, 18, and 19, 1980

Appendix 3. Peck Concerti with the Chicago Symphony Orchestra

Year	Date	Qty.	Piece Performed	Conductor	Venue
1960	Nov. 24, 25	2	Bach: Suite in b minor	Fritz Reiner	Orchestra Hall
1961	Feb. 5	1	Bach: Brandenburg Concerto No. 5	Lukas Foss	Television
1961	Nov. 2, 3	2	Bach: Brandenburg Concerto No. 4	Hans Rosbaud	Television
1963	Apr. 11, 12	2	Mozart: Concerto for flute and harp	Fritz Reiner	Orchestra Hall
1963	May 11	1	Mozart: Concerto for flute and harp	Walter Hendl	Cedar Rapids, Iowa
1963	July 1	1	Bach: Brandenburg Concerto No. 5	Lukas Foss	Ravinia Festival
1964	Mar. 12, 13	2	Martinu: Concerto for flute and violin	Jean Martinon	Orchestra Hall
1964	May 2	1	Mozart: Concerto for flute and harp	Walter Hendl	Orchestra Hall
1966	Jan. 27, 28	2	Gesensway: Flute Concerto	Hans Schmidt-Isserstedt	Orchestra Hall
1966	Feb.–Apr.	20	Martin: Concerto for seven winds	Jean Martinon	Orchestra Hall and on tour
1966	June 9	1	Vivaldi: Flute Concerto in g minor	Antonio Janigro	Orchestra Hall
1966	June 16, 17	2	Bach: Brandenburg Concerti nos. 2, 4, and 5	Jean Martinon	Orchestra Hall
1966	July 10	1	Martinu: Concerto for flute and violin	Seiji Ozawa	Ravinia Festival
1966	July 31	1	Berio: Serenata for flute and fourteen instruments	Seiji Ozawa	Ravinia Festival
1966	Sept. 26	1	Foss: Elytres for flute and orchestra	Lukas Foss	University of Chicago
1967	Jan. 14, 16	2	Hanson: Serenade for flute and strings	Morton Gould	Orchestra Hall and Chicago Heights, Ill.

Year	Date	Qty.	Piece Performed	Conductor	Venue
1967	June 1, 4	2	Bach: Triple Concerto in a minor	Jean Martinon	Orchestra Hall and Dearborn, Mich.
1967	June 3, 4	2	Bach: Suite in b minor	Jean Martinon	Orchestra Hall and Dearborn, Mich.
1967	June 8, 11, 19	3	Vivaldi: Flute Concerto, Op. 10 No. 3 in D Major	Antonio Janigro	Orchestra Hall and Madison, Wisc.
1967	June 10, 21	2	Telemann: Concerto in D Major	Antonio Janigro	Orchestra Hall and Madison, Wisc.
1968	July 22, 23	2	Griffes: Poem	Aaron Copland	Ravinia Festival
1969	Mar. 11	1	Bach: Brandenburg Concerti Nos. 2 and 5	Margaret Hillis	Orchestra Hall
1969	May 17	1	Nielsen: Concerto for flute	Irwin Hoffman	Orchestra Hall
1969	June 3	1	Bach: Suite in b minor	Irwin Hoffman	University of Chicago
1969	July 6	1	Bach: Brandenburg Concerto No. 2	Seiji Ozawa	Ravinia Festival
1969	July 13	1	Vivaldi: Flute Concerto in g minor	Antonio Janigro	Ravinia Festival
1970	Jan. 22, 23	2	Van Vlijmen: Serenata	Bruno Maderna	Orchestra Hall
1970	Jan. 24	1	Bach: Brandenburg Concerto No. 4	Margaret Hillis	Orchestra Hall
1970	June 15	1	Mozart: Concerto for flute and harp	Irwin Hoffman	Orchestra Hall
1971	July 8	1	Mozart: Concerto for flute and harp	Seiji Ozawa	Ravinia Festival
1971	Nov. 6	1	Bloch: Concertino for flute and viola	Henry Mazer	Orchestra Hall
1972	Jan. 15	1	Bach: Suite in b minor	Szymon Goldberg	Orchestra Hall
1972	Jan. 27–31, Feb. 7	5	Ghedini: Sonata da Concerto	Carlo Maria Giulini	Orchestra Hall, Milwaukee, Wisc., and DeKalb, Ill.
1973	Feb. 15, 16	2	Diamond: Elegies for flute and English horn	Henry Mazer	Orchestra Hall

Year	Date	Qty.	Piece Performed	Conductor	Venue
1974	July 27	1	Bach: Suite in b minor	Kazimierzi Kord	Ravinia Festival
1975	June 29	1	Bach: Brandenburg Concerti Nos. 2, 4, and 5	James Levine	Ravinia Festival
1975	July 20	1	Mozart: Concerto in D Major	James Levine	Ravinia Festival
1975	Nov. 6, 7, 9	3	Mozart: Concerto in G Major	Raphael Kubelik	Orchestra Hall
1976	Mar. 31	1	Chaminade: Concertino	Henry Mazer	Orchestra Hall
1976	June 26	1	Bach: Brandenburg Concerti Nos. 2, 4, and 5	James Levine	Ravinia Festival
1977	July 10	1	Bach: Brandenburg Concerti Nos. 2, 4, and 5	James Levine	Ravinia Festival
1977	Sept. 20, 23–25	4	Mozart: Concerto for flute and harp	Henry Mazer	Rockford, Quincy, Macomb, and Urbana, Ill.
1977	Nov. 5, 9, 14	3	Mozart: Concerto for flute and harp	Henry Mazer	West Point, N.Y., and Orchestra Hall
1979	Oct. 4, 6, 8, 16	4	Mozart: Concerto in D Major	Sir Georg Solti	Orchestra Hall and Milwaukee, Wisc.
1980	June 22	1	Telemann: Suite in a minor	James Levine	Ravinia Festival
1982	Dec. 2, 3, 5, 6	4	Barber: *Capricorn* concerto	Raphael Kubelik	Orchestra Hall and Milwaukee, Wisc.
1983	May 11–13, 15	4	Telemann: Suite in a minor	Leonard Slatkin	Orchestra Hall
1984	June 15	1	Vivaldi (Rousseau): *Le printemps* for solo flute	Christopher Hogwood	Orchestra Hall
1985	Apr. 18–20	3	Gould: Concerto (world premiere)	Sir Georg Solti	Orchestra Hall
1986	Sept. 17–20	4	Mozart: Concerto in D Major	Yoshimi Takeda	Urbana, Decatur, and Peoria, Ill., and Madison, Wisc.
1991	Mar. 28–30	3	Mozart: Concerto in G Major	Sir Georg Solti	Orchestra Hall

Year	Date	Qty.	Piece Performed	Conductor	Venue
1992	Mar. 5, 6, 8, 10	4	Martin: Concerto for seven winds	Erich Leinsdorf	Orchestra Hall
1993	July 10	1	Bach: Brandenburg Concerto no. 5	Tibor Pesek	Ravinia Festival
1994	June 11, 14, 16–18	5	Mozart: Concerto in G Major	Mark Wigglesworth	Orchestra Hall
1998	Dec. 17–20	4	Nielsen: Concerto for flute	Daniel Barenboim	Orchestra Hall

Appendix 4. Non–Chicago Symphony Solo Dates

Year	Performing with	Music Performed
1949	Seattle Symphony	Mozart: Concerto in D Major
1952	U.S. Marine Symphony	Telemann: Suite in a minor
1953	U.S. Marine Symphony	Mozart: Concerto for flute and harp (Pedicord)
1955	U.S. Marine Symphony	Griffes: Poem
1955	U.S. Marine Symphony	Barber: *Capricorn* concerto
1957	Kansas City Philharmonic	Mozart: Concerto for flute and harp (Lee Swinson), three performances
1957	Santa Fe Chamber Orchestra	Bach: Brandenburg Concerto no. 4, two performances
1957	Park College, Mo., Chamber Ens.	Telemann: Suite in a minor
1957	Park College, Mo., Chamber Ens.	Bach: Brandenburg Concerto no. 4
1957	Santa Fe Chamber Orchestra	Mozart: Concerto for flute and harp (Lee Swinson)
1958	Park College, Mo., Chamber Ens.	Bach: Suite no. 2; and Hanson: Serenade
1959	Saint Joseph, Mo., Symphony	Mozart: Concerto in G Major, and Kennan: Night Soliloquy
1962	Chicago Orchestra Ensemble	Bach: Brandenburg Concerto no. 5
1963	Gary, Indiana, Symphony	Mozart: Concerto for flute and harp (Edward Druzinsky)
1963	Sinfonia Chicago	Stein: Rhapsody
1965	Charlotte, N.C., Symphony	Mozart: Concerto for flute and harp (Edward Druzinsky)
1966	Grant Park Symphony, Chicago	Mozart: Concerto for flute and harp (Edward Druzinsky)
1966	Evanston, Ill., Symphony	Mozart: Concerto for flute and harp (Edward Druzinsky)
1967	Greenville, S.C., Symphony	Mozart: Concerto for flute and harp (Edward Druzinsky)
1967	Benton Harbor, Mich., Symphony	Mozart: Concerto for flute and harp (Edward Druzinsky)
1968	Chattanooga, Tenn., Symphony	Mozart: Concerto for flute and harp (Edward Druzinsky)
1968	Chattanooga, Tenn., Symphony	Hanson: Serenade

Year	Performing with	Music Performed
1968	Skokie Valley, Ill., Symphony	Mozart: Concerto for flute and harp (Edward Druzinsky)
1968	Chicago South Side Symphony	Mozart: Concerto for flute and harp (Edward Druzinsky)
1970	Erie, Pa., Philharmonic	Mozart: Concerto for flute and harp (Edward Druzinsky)
1970	Carmel, Calif., Bach Festival Orchestra	Mozart: Concerto for flute and harp (Anne Adams)
1970	Oak Park, Ill., Symphony	Mozart: Concerto for flute and harp (Edward Druzinsky)
1971	Carmel, Calif., Bach Festival Orchestra	Mozart: Concerto in D Major, two performances
1972	Australian Radio Orchestra	Mozart: Concerto in G Major
1973	Lake Forest, Ill., Symphony	Mozart: Concerto for flute and harp (Edward Druzinsky)
1974	Alton, Ill., Symphony	Mozart: Concerto for flute and harp (Edward Druzinsky)
1976	Hinsdale, Ill., Symphony	Mozart: Concerto for flute and harp (Edward Druzinsky)
1976	Oak Park, Ill., Symphony	Nielsen: Concerto for flute
1978	Rockford, Ill., Symphony	Mozart: Concerto in D Major
1978	Gold Coast Chamber Orchestra, Chicago	Telemann: Suite in a minor
1978	Waterloo, Iowa, Philharmonic	Mozart: Concerto for flute and harp (Edward Druzinsky), two performances
1979	Webster, Mo., Symphony	Mozart: Concerto in D Major
1979	Carmel, Calif., Bach Festival Orchestra	Telemann: Suite in a minor, two performances
1980	Skokie Valley, Ill., Symphony	Mozart: Concerto for flute and harp (Edward Druzinsky)
1981	Evanston, Ill., Symphony	Mozart: Concerto for flute and harp (Edward Druzinsky)
1982	Elmhurst, Ill., Symphony	Mozart: Concerto for flute and harp (Edward Druzinsky)
1983	Northbrook, Ill., Symphony	Mozart: Concerto in D Major
1983	Victoria, Canada, Festival Orchestra	Mozart: Concerto in D Major
1983	Elmhurst, Ill., Symphony	Chaminade: Concertino; and Poulenc: Sonata and Concerto
1984	Sinfonia Chicago	Mozart: Concerto in D Major
1984	Ferris Chorale Orchestra, Chicago	Hanson: Serenade

Year	Performing with	Music Performed
1985	Lynchburg, Va., Symphony	Mozart: Concerto in G Major
1988	Madison, Wisc., Symphony	Mozart: Concerto for flute and harp (Edward Druzinsky)
1989	Salinas, Calif., Monterey Symphony	Gould: Concerto
1989	Carmel, Calif., Monterey Symphony	Gould: Concerto
1989	Monterey, Calif., Symphony	Gould: Concerto
1989	Kalamazoo, Mich., Symphony	Gould: Concerto
1989	Aurora, Ill. (Fox Valley Symphony)	Mozart: Concerto in D Major; and Griffes: Poem
1989	Highland Park, Ill., Symphony	Mozart: Concerto in D Major; and Bach: Brandenburg Concerto no. 4
1991	Highland Park, Ill., Symphony	Mozart: Concerto for flute and harp (Edward Druzinsky)
1991	St. Joseph, Mich., Symphony	Mozart: Concerto in D Major and Andante in C Major
1993	DePaul Univ., Chicago, Symphony	Mozart: Concerto for flute and harp (Edward Druzinsky)
1993	Highland Park, Ill., Symphony	Mozart: Concerto for flute and harp (Edward Druzinsky)
1993	Highland Park, Ill., Symphony	Telemann: Suite in a minor
1994	Kansas City, Mo., NFA Symphony	Gould: Concerto
1996	Woodstock, Ill., Chamber Symphony	Mozart: Concerto in D Major, two performances
1998	Topeka, Kans., Symphony	Mozart: Concerto in G Major
1999	Woodstock, Ill., Chamber Symphony	Mozart: Concerto for flute and harp (Sarah Bullen), two performances
1999	Northbrook, Ill., Symphony	Mozart: Concerto in G Major
1999	Biloxi, Miss., Gulf Coast Symphony	Mozart Concerto in D Major
2000	Central Mich. Univ., De Paul Univ. Concert Band	Badings: Concerto for flute and wind ensemble
2000	Chicago, DePaul Univ. Concert Band	Badings: Concerto for flute and wind ensemble
2001	Park Ridge, Ill., Symphony	Grier: Concerto for flute

Index

Note: Page numbers in *italics* indicate photographs.

New York Philharmonic Orchestra, 16, 37, 135
New Yorker, 24–25
Nielsen, Carl, 99
Nielsen Flute Concerto, *58*
A Night on Bare Mountain (Mussorgsky), 3
Nilsson, Birgit, 76
Nocturnes (Debussy), 106–107
Norman, Jesse, 75
Northbrook Symphony Orchestra, 121
Nucci, Leo, 83

Oboe Concerto (Strauss), 123
Oistrakh, David, 92
Okura Hotel, 33
Oldberg, Eric, 4–5, 23
Opava, Emil, 93
opera, 75–80, 81–87, 129, 135. *See also specific opera companies*
Orchestra Hall: acoustics, 98–99, 104, 110–11; and opera, 76, 79, 81–82; and recordings, 98–99, 100; renovations, 110–11; and solo dates, 114, 119
Orchestra Seminar, 130
Ormandy, Eugene, 17, *59, 62*
Otello (Verdi), 77, 83–84
outside jobs, 124–34
Ozawa, Seiji: concerto performances, *53;* and Levine, 19; and the Ravinia Festival, 18; and recordings, 98–101, 131; and solo dates, 114; tenure with the CSO, 1

Palais de Beaux Arts, 51
Pape, Rene, 110
Paray, Paul, 96
Paris, France, 37, 50–51
Paris Orchestra, 16
Pavarotti, Luciano, 83–84
Peck, Donald: and the Curtis Institute of Music, 93; with Duchess of Kent, *56;* final recording session, 111; with friends, *57;* at home, *59;* and the Morton Gould Flute Concerto, *56,* 115–17; Mozart Concerto performance, *53;* and the Nielsen Flute Concerto, *58;* promotional poster, *54;* with Solti, *58*
Perlman, Itzhak, 91, 109–10

Perth, Australia, 30–31
Pertusi, Michele, 79
Peters, Roberta, 84
Petrillo, James, 4
Petrouchka (Stravinsky), 100, 103
Philadelphia Orchestra, 21, 63, 64, 70, 93, 135
Philharmonie am Gasteig, 41, 42
Phillips, Paul, 31, 34–36
Pictures at an Exhibition (Mussorgsky), 3, 46, 96, 105–106
Les Pieds du Cochon (restaurant), 36
Pikler, Charles, 57
platinum flutes, 90–91
Polaski, Deborah, 78, 107
Pons, Lily, 84
pop singers, 86
Popp, Lucia, 49
practice time, 125, 133
Prado museum, 36
Prelude to the Afternoon of a Faun (Debussy), 7–8, 29, 66, 106–107, 122
Pretre, George, 99
Previn, André, 64, 70, 74, 103
Previtali, Fernando, 70–71
Pribaltiskaya Hotel, 34
Price, Leontyne, 87, 96
private teaching, 125
Progress Press, 123
Prokofiev, Sergei, 14–15, 92–93, 96
publishing, 116, 121–23
Puccini, Giacomo, 49–50
Puerto Rico, 127–28

Rampal, Jean-Pierre, 90–91
Rand, Lola, 122
Rapier, Wayne, 121
Rattle, Simon, 11
Ravel, Joseph-Maurice, 67, 98, 107–108
Raven, Seymour, 5
Ravinia Festival: and chief conductors, 1; concerto performances, *53;* and Eschenbach, 20–21; and guest conductors, 60, 61, 68, 69; and Münch, 66; and opera, 78, 81, 84–85; and Orchestra Hall renovations, 111; and outside jobs, 131; and solo dates, 114, 119; and staff conductors, 17–20, 20–21
RCA Corporation, 60, 69, 95–100, 102–106, 112

Donald Peck is principal flute emeritus of the Chicago Symphony Orchestra. He served under four music directors, toured the world with the orchestra, and made three hundred recordings. He is noted as an orchestral soloist and recitalist. He is currently on the faculty of Roosevelt University in Chicago.